# EXTENDING SCIENCE

## SCIENCE

**15**

# FOOD

## Selected Topics

**E N Ramsden** BSc, PhD, DPhil

**Stanley Thornes (Publishers) Ltd**

First published in 1988 by
Stanley Thornes (Publishers) Ltd
Old Station Drive
Leckhampton
CHELTENHAM GL53 0DN
England

British Library Cataloguing in Publication Data

Ramsden, E.N.
    Food — (Extending science).
    1. Food.
    I. Title    II. Series
    641.3

    ISBN 0-85950-820-X

Typeset by Tech-Set, Gateshead, Tyne & Wear.
Printed and bound in Great Britain by Ebenezer Baylis & Son, Worcester.

# CONTENTS

# PREFACE

The *Extending Science* series began as a set of books covering material which is an extension of normal syllabus work and omitting core material which is in text books. The books deal with social, economic, environmental and technological aspects of science. Since the series began, these aspects of science have been incorporated in the national criteria for GCSE science and have become part of mainstream examination science. The Extending Science series is finding application in the new modular science courses.

I consulted the GCSE Modular Science syllabuses before selecting the content of *Food*, but, in order to keep the book short, I have omitted items such as digestion, minerals, vitamins, food tests and well-known experiments. I ask teachers to refer pupils to text books for this basic material. The debate on diet and health is so topical that I have included more than the syllabuses dictate. A feature of this area is that it affords opportunities for readers to improve their skills in data analysis. I have addressed the question of why millions of people are hungry in a world which grows enough food to feed everyone. Although this is too difficult a question to receive an answer, I think that children should begin to consider it. Some of the contributions of the food industry to the manufacture, processing and preservation of foodstuffs have been described, and recent developments in the labelling of packaged foods and the use of food additives have been included.

E N Ramsden
1988

# ACKNOWLEDGEMENTS

The author and publishers are grateful to the following for supplying photographs and drawings and giving permission for reproduction:

Chatto and Windus (p. 70)
Compassion in World Farming (p. 21)
Holt Studios Ltd (cover)
ICI Billingham (pp. 3, 4)
J Sainsbury plc (p. 33)
Keith Anderson, Studio K Photography (cover, pp. 2, 3, 5, 6, 10, 17, 37, 40–1, 62, 77–9, 82–4)
Meat and Livestock Commission (p. 41)
National Dairy Council (p. 65)
Slimmer Clubs Ltd (p. 5)
Stilton Cheese Manufacturers Association (p. 30)
The Wine Institute of California (p. 49)
Times Newspapers Ltd © (p. 74)
Tweedy of Burnley (p. 56)
United Distillers plc (p. 50)

Thanks are also due to the following for giving permission to reproduce written material:

Consumers Association (p. 82)
Chatto and Windus (p. 22)
*Daily Telegraph* (pp. 29, 45)
*The Independent* (p. 31)
*The Sunday Times* (p. 81)

The book *Food Tables* by A E Bender and D A Bender (OUP, 1986) has been an invaluable source of data.

# WHY DO WE NEED FOOD?

Why do they need food?

They need food

- to build new tissues
- to repair damaged tissues, such as cuts and broken bones
- to supply the energy which they need for all their activities.

All foods are chemical compounds. There are three main classes of foods: carbohydrates, proteins and fats. In addition, we need mineral salts, vitamins and water.

## CARBOHYDRATES

**Carbohydrates** contain the elements carbon, hydrogen and oxygen. **Sugars**, **starches** and **cellulose** are the carbohydrates that are important in our diet. The starch in our diet comes from cereals, e.g. wheat and rice, from pulses (the seeds of legumes, e.g. peas and beans) and from 'root' crops, e.g. potatoes, yams and cassava. Most of the sugar in our diet is **sucrose** (table sugar). It is present in fruits and in many manufactured foods, e.g. cakes, biscuits, jams and soft drinks.

Carbohydrates are often the cheapest foods and therefore the main source of energy. Energy is measured in joules (J) and kilojoules (kJ); 1 kJ = 1000 J. Sometimes, the older unit, the calorie, is used; 1 calorie = 4.2 J. In respiration, carbohydrates are oxidised to carbon dioxide and water. The energy released is about 17 kJ per gram of carbohydrate.

$$\text{glucose} + \text{oxygen} \longrightarrow \text{carbon dioxide} + \text{water;}$$
$$\text{energy is released}$$

If we eat more carbohydrates than we need for our short term energy needs, the liver turns the excess into either glycogen or fat. Glycogen is stored in the liver or the muscles. Fat is stored in fat deposits round the kidneys and under the skin.

The cell walls of all plant tissues are made of the carbohydrate called **cellulose**. Mammals have no enzymes for digesting cellulose. Sheep and cows can feed on it because cellulose-digesting bacteria in their guts digest it for them. Humans cannot digest cellulose (although bacteria in the human colon digest part of the cellulose). Nevertheless, we need cellulose in our diet as it prevents constipation by providing **dietary fibre** or **roughage**. Dietary fibre adds bulk to the food and increases its ability to retain water. A moist, bulky mass of food is easier for muscles to work against as they keep food moving through the alimentary canal. The results of eating a diet low in fibre are described on p. 17.

**These foods are rich in carbohydrates**

## PROTEINS

Proteins are compounds which contain carbon, hydrogen, oxygen, nitrogen and usually sulphur. Every protein molecule is made from a large number of molecules of **amino acids**. Twenty different amino acids are found in proteins.

Plants can build all the amino acids they need from carbohydrates and nitrates. Animals cannot do this: they obtain their amino acids from proteins in plants and in the flesh of other animals. In digestion, proteins are broken down into amino acids. These are transported round the body in the blood stream. In the tissues, amino acids are used to build a variety of proteins.

Table 1.1   **Where we obtain protein**

| Sources of animal protein | Sources of plant protein |
| --- | --- |
| Lean meat | Nuts |
| Fish | Cereals |
| Egg white | Pulses (seeds of legumes – |
| Milk and cheese | peas, beans, lentils (etc.) |

These foods are sources of protein

Amino acids cannot be stored in the body. If we eat more protein than we need, the body converts the excess of protein into carbohydrates. These are either oxidised to provide energy or converted into fat and stored.

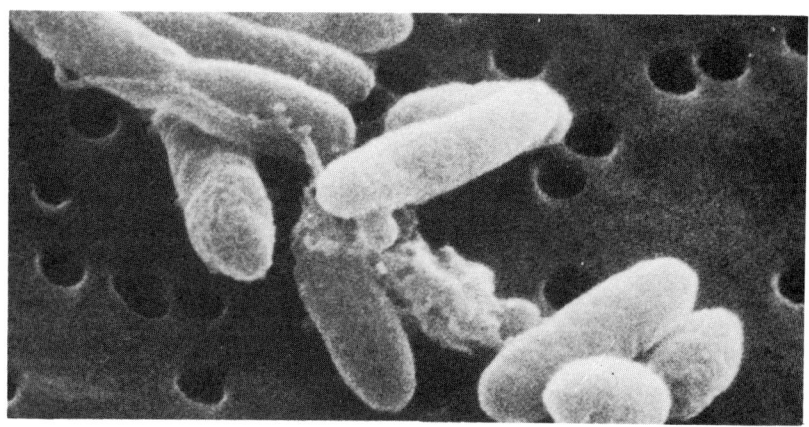

*Methylophilus methylotrophus* (magnified many times)

ICI has developed a method of using a micro-organism to manufacture protein. The micro-organism, *Methylophilus methylotrophus*, is shown above. It is grown in a large container called a *fermenter*. Methanol, mineral salts and ammonia are pumped into the fermenter. The micro-organism feeds on these nutrients and multiplies: it doubles in mass every 2 hours. After 30 hours, the micro-organism is *harvested*: it is separated from the liquid. The product is dried and converted into granules. ICI call their product **Pruteen**. It contains about 70% protein and has been used successfully as a feedstuff for animals.

The ICI fermenter at Billingham is 50 m high and 7 m wide

## FATS AND OILS

Fats and oils are compounds of carbon, hydrogen and oxygen. Fats are solids; they occur in animal products, e.g. meat and milk. Oils are liquids; they occur in plants and animals. We use plant oils for cooking and for making margarine.

Table 1.2  **Sources of fats and oils**

| *Animal sources of fats and oils* | *Plant sources of oils* |
| --- | --- |
| Meat | Seeds of plants, e.g. |
| Milk, cheese, butter | sunflower seeds |
| Margarine | Nuts, e.g. peanuts |
| Egg yolk | Olives |

Fats and oils are used by the body to form cell membranes and other structures. They also provide energy. In respiration, fats and oils are oxidised to carbon dioxide and water with the release of energy (37 kJ/g).

Since fats can be stored in the body, they provide a reserve of energy which can be used when needed. The deposits of fat under the skin form an insulating layer which reduces heat loss from the body. People in tropical countries therefore need to eat less fat than people in cold countries. The average Briton eats 80–150 g of fats and oils per day. When people constantly eat more fats and oils than they need for energy, the stored fat leads to *obesity* or being *overweight*.

Foods that contain fats and oils

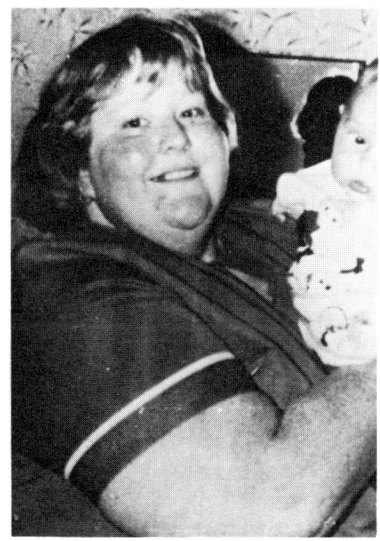

Obesity: before and after a controlled diet.

## Saturated and unsaturated fats

Fats are compounds of carbon, hydrogen and oxygen. Molecules of fats contain long chains of carbon atoms, to which hydrogen atoms are bonded:

$$H - \overset{\overset{\displaystyle H}{|}}{\underset{\underset{\displaystyle H}{|}}{C}} - \overset{\overset{\displaystyle H}{|}}{\underset{\underset{\displaystyle H}{|}}{C}} - \overset{\overset{\displaystyle H}{|}}{\underset{\underset{\displaystyle H}{|}}{C}} - \overset{\overset{\displaystyle H}{|}}{\underset{\underset{\displaystyle H}{|}}{C}} - \overset{\overset{\displaystyle H}{|}}{\underset{\underset{\displaystyle H}{|}}{C}} -$$

*part of a saturated fat*

When there are only single bonds between the carbon atoms, a compound is described as **saturated**. A compound which has a double bond between carbon atoms is described as **unsaturated**:

$$
\begin{array}{ccccccccc}
 & H & & H & & H & & H & & H \\
 & | & & | & & | & & | & & | \\
H - & C & - & C & = & C & - & C & - & C & - \\
 & | & & & & & & | & & | \\
 & H & & & & & & H & & H
\end{array}
$$
*part of an unsaturated fat*

If there is more than one double bond in the molecule, a compound is described as **polyunsaturated**:

$$
\begin{array}{ccccccccccccccccc}
 & H & & H & & H & & H & & H & & H & & H & & H & & H \\
 & | & & | & & | & & | & & | & & | & & | & & | & & | \\
H - & C & - & C & = & C & - & C & = & C & - & C & - & C & = & C & - & C & - \\
 & | & & & & & & & & & & | & & & & & & | \\
 & H & & & & & & & & & & H & & & & & & H
\end{array}
$$

*part of a polyunsaturated fat*

Saturated and unsaturated fats behave differently. The theory that eating a lot of saturated fats makes a person likely to develop heart disease is discussed on p. 18.

'High in polyunsaturates'

## MINERAL SALTS

We need small quantities of mineral salts in our diet (see Table 2.6, p. 25). Salts which some people lack in their diets are:

iron salts
- essential for the manufacture of red blood cells; a shortage causes anaemia
- obtained from red meat, eggs, spinach and other vegetables

calcium salts
- essential for the formation of bones and teeth
- obtained from cheese and milk.

## VITAMINS

Vitamins are substances which are required by the body in small quantities. They are not digested and not used as a source of energy. They work with enzymes to enable chemical reactions to take place in the cells. Vitamins which may be lacking in some diets are:

vitamin B12 – present in meat, fish and dairy products. A shortage causes anaemia.

vitamin C   – present in fresh fruits and vegetables. A shortage lowers a person's resistance to infection, and a severe shortage causes scurvy (bleeding gums).

vitamin D   – present in foods containing fats and oils. A severe shortage causes rickets (soft bones in children, fragile bones in adults).

Some of the nutritional value of food is lost when it is cooked. When food is boiled, the group of vitamins called B vitamins and vitamin C dissolve in the cooking water. These vitamins are partially destroyed by the high temperature. When vegetables are boiled, enzymes in their cells attack the vitamin C. If vegetables are plunged straight into boiling water, these enzymes are destroyed and less vitamin C is lost. To avoid losing vitamins, you should use as little water as possible, boil the water before you add the vegetables and stop as soon as they are sufficiently cooked. Vitamin A and vitamin D are soluble in fats and are not dissolved out by water or destroyed by heat. Mineral salts also dissolve out of food into the cooking water.

## WATER

Water is an essential part of our diet. About 70 per cent of most body tissues consists of water. By sweating, urinating and breathing, we lose 2–3 litres of water a day. To replace the lost water, we drink about 1.5 litres a day and take in the rest as part of our food. A person can live for 2–3 weeks without solid food but will die in 2–3 days without water.

# COMPOSITION OF SOME FOODS

The figure shows the percentages of carbohydrate, protein, fat, water and fibre in some foods.

The percentage composition of some foods

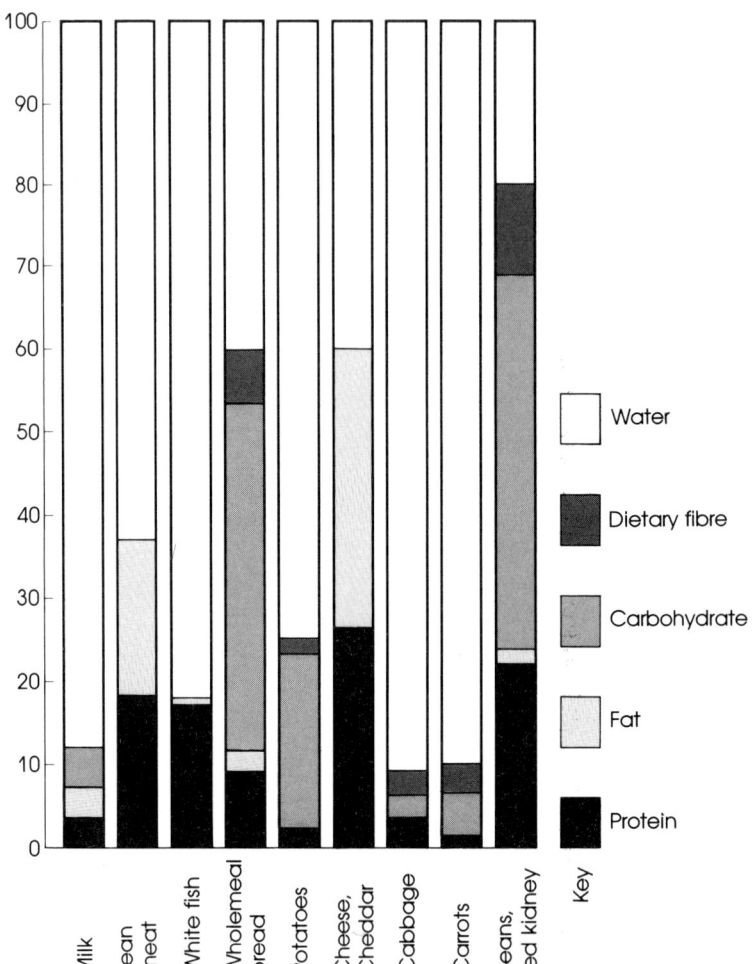

---

**EXPERIMENT 1**

## Some food tests

You can test samples of food, e.g. potato, bread, egg yolk, egg white, to find out what food materials they contain. Refer to a text book for details of food tests.

---

**EXPERIMENT 2**

## Is vitamin C lost on cooking?

Vegetables are often boiled in large volumes of water. Then the cooking water is thrown away. Does this method involve a loss of nutritious vitamin C?

1) You need a solution of vitamin C. (Use either fresh lemon juice or a solution of a 1 g tablet of vitamin C from the pharmacist.) You need a solution of DCPIP (40 mg of phenolindo-2,6-dichlorophenol in 100 cm³ of water).

2) How to compare the vitamin C content of different solutions: With a teat pipette, add DCPIP solution drop by drop to 1 cm³ of a solution of vitamin C. The dye will be decolourised. Note the number of drops of dye that can be decolourised by the vitamin C solution. The number of drops of DCPIP solution is proportional to the concentration of vitamin C in the solution.

3) Plan an experiment to find out how the concentration of vitamin C changes when you boil a solution of vitamin C for 0, 5, 10, 15 and 20 minutes.

4) Plan an experiment to find out how the vitamin C content of cooking water changes when you add Brussels sprouts (or cabbage) to boiling water and boil for 0, 5, 10, 15 and 20 minutes.

Obtain your teacher's approval before you do your experiments.

---

**EXPERIMENT 3**

## Compare the vitamin C content of some drinks

1) Assemble some fruit juices and fruit drinks, e.g. fresh orange juice, canned grapefruit juice, lemonade. You also need a 0.1% solution of DCPIP.

2) As you saw in Experiment 2, this blue dye is decolourised by vitamin C. Think up an experiment using the dye solution to compare the vitamin C content of the different drinks. Check out your plan with your teacher before you put it into practice.

---

**EXPERIMENT 4**

## Testing the cooking water

Lentils, haricot beans, butter beans, mung beans and red kidney beans all have a high content of iron compounds. Plan an experiment to find out whether iron compounds dissolve out into the cooking water.

To test for iron salts, add 5 cm³ of the test solution (equal volumes of 1% solutions of potassium hexacyanoferrate(II) and hydrochloric acid). A blue precipitate shows the presence of an iron salt.

When you have planned your experiment, obtain your teacher's approval before you start work.

## QUESTIONS ON CHAPTER 1

**1** The items shown below contain carbohydrates, fats, proteins, minerals, vitamins and water. Say which one or two of these classes of compounds are found in important quantities in each item. (For example, meat contains chiefly protein and fat.)

Some foods

**2** (a) Some people claim to feel fit on a diet of raw fruit and vegetables. What is the advantage of eating these foods uncooked?
  (b) What is the advantage of cooking vegetables in the steam from boiling water, rather than in the water itself?

**3** Does a person who does hard physical work need a lot of (a) protein, (b) carbohydrate, (c) fat? Explain your answer.

**4** (a) Why must all diets contain some protein?
  (b) Is it better to eat a large amount of protein at one meal or regular, small amounts of protein? Explain your answer.

**5** (a) If you want to eat a snack between meals, do you eat an apple or a bar of chocolate? Explain your choice.

(b) If you are preparing for a long hike, and you want to take a sustaining snack, do you take an apple or a bar of chocolate? Explain your choice.

## CROSSWORD ON FOOD

Trace or photocopy the grid (see note on p. ii), and then fill in the answers to the clues.

### Across

1 Needed in your diet in small quantities (8)
7 If your diet contains these, you will have energy (13)
8 Part of a loaf (5)
9 See 13 across
10 These are liquid 11 across (4)
11 Provide energy and warmth (4)
13, 9 across. Do this to obtain nourishment (3, 4)
14 The process of breaking down foods (9)

### Down

2 If you live in this part of the world, you will need to eat fat (5)
3 Potatoes are grown as a ____ ____ (4, 4)
4 Same clue as 1 across (8)
5 The process of oxidising foods (11)
6 Needed in the diet to repair tissues (8)
7 This kind of 7 across adds dietary fibre (9)
12 This mixed-up diet has no D (3)

**CHAPTER**

# 2

# WHAT IS A BALANCED DIET?

A 'balanced' diet is one which contains

- enough carbohydrates and fats to meet the need for energy
- enough protein of the right kind to provide the essential amino acids
- vitamins, mineral salts, plant fibre and water.

## HOW MUCH ENERGY MUST THE DIET PROVIDE?

The graph below shows how much energy people of different ages and occupations need. The figures are average values: people differ in their energy needs. The units are kilojoules per day (kJ/day).

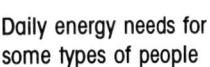
Daily energy needs for some types of people

Energy is obtained from carbohydrates, fats and proteins. The total energy in the diet must keep the body processes working, keep the body warm and meet the needs of work and other activities. The next graph shows some average figures for the energy used in various activities.

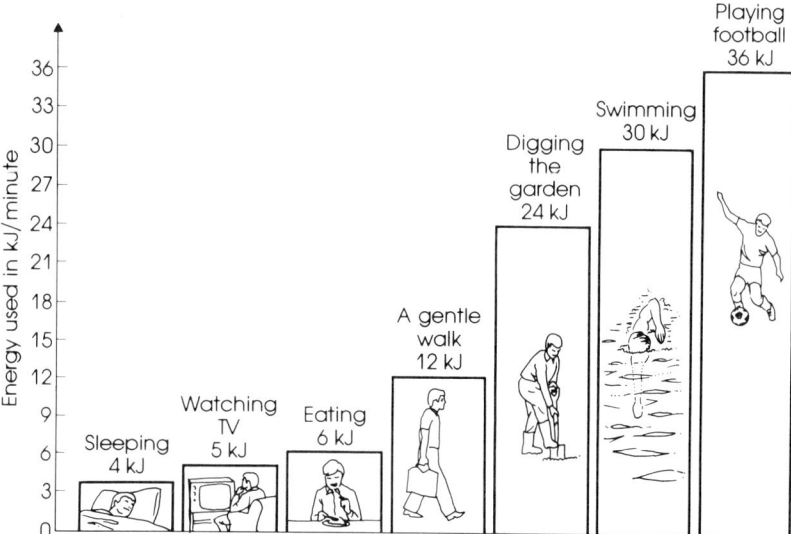

Energy used per minute in various activites

# HOW MUCH PROTEIN MUST THE DIET CONTAIN?

A human adult needs about 0.6 g of protein per kg of body weight per day. This is about 40 g of protein a day for a fairly active man of average weight. He could get this from 200 g (7 oz) of lean meat or 500 g of bread or 2 kg of potatoes. Growing children need more protein per kg of body weight. A shortage of protein prevents children from growing to their proper size, and a severe shortage may make a child mentally retarded. Pregnant women have a special need for protein.

Table 2.1   Amount of protein needed daily per kg of body weight (average values)

| Type of person | Amount of protein needed daily (g/kg of body weight) |
| --- | --- |
| Man | 0.6 |
| Woman | 0.6 |
| Pregnant woman | 0.8 |
| Breast-feeding mother | 1.2 |
| Baby | 1.5 |
| Child | 1.0 |
| Adolescent | 0.7 |

## A few questions

Table 2.2 on p. 14 shows the protein content of some foods. Table 2.1 gives average values of the amounts of protein needed by different types of people. Use the tables to answer the following questions.

**Table 2.2  Protein content of some foods (in percentage by weight)**

| Food | Percentage of protein |
| --- | --- |
| Beans, kidney | 22 |
| Bread, white | 7.8 |
| Bread, wholemeal | 8.8 |
| Cheese (Cheddar) | 26 |
| Fish (white) | 18 |
| Meat (lean) | 16 |
| Milk (whole) | 3.3 |
| Potatoes | 2.0 |

1)  How much cheese does a 39 kg adolescent need to eat in a day to satisfy her need for protein if this is her only source of protein?

2)  How much lean meat does a 50 kg pregnant woman need to eat in a day if this is her only source of protein?

3)  How much milk would a baby of 4.4 kg need to drink each day to supply all the protein he needs? Assume this is his only source of protein.

4)  How much wholemeal bread would a child of 16 kg weight need to eat in one day to provide him with enough protein?

5)  What weight of kidney beans would a 44 kg adolescent need to eat to provide one day's requirement of protein?

# HOW MUCH DO WE NEED OF VITAMINS, MINERALS AND FIBRE?

We need only small quantities of vitamins and minerals. Table 2.6, p. 25 gives some figures. We need 30 g of fibre daily (see p. 26).

# SPECIAL DIETARY NEEDS

Some people have special dietary needs:

- Milk is a complete diet for a new-born baby; see p. 63.
- Pregnant women need to be sure that their diet contains enough protein, calcium, iron and vitamins to feed the developing fetus.
- Mothers who are breast-feeding their babies need much more protein and calcium than a normal diet provides. If the mother is short of calcium, calcium compounds will be withdrawn from her bones to supply the baby with the calcium it needs. She needs 1.6–2.0 g of calcium per day.

- Children need more protein per kg of body weight than adults. Children are growing and need protein to build new tissues. If a child is fed large amounts of starchy foods, such as maize and rice, it will feel full without having eaten enough protein. It can be undernourished without being hungry. On your television screens, you have seen children who look tired and miserable and have swollen abdomens. These children are suffering from **kwashiorkor**, a disease caused by severe lack of protein.

## UNBALANCED DIETS

Examples of unbalanced diets are:

- Diets which lack protein: diets based largely on starchy foods, e.g. yam, cassava, maize and banana contain too little protein.
- Diets which lack vitamins: diets based largely on maize and rice may contain too little vitamin A (from green vegetables) and vitamins B1 and B3.
- Diets which do not even provide enough energy. Many people in Asia and South America can obtain only enough food to provide about 9000 kJ per day. This gives them enough energy to stay alive but not enough to do a day's work.
- Diets which lack dietary fibre: diets which are low in cereals and vegetables are unhealthy; they are discussed under 'Western diet'.

## 'WESTERN DIET'

What people mean by the *Western diet* is that eaten by most people in the rich, industrial continents of the world: Europe, North America, the USSR and Australasia (see map on p. 68).

In the rich countries, most people can afford to eat a diet which gives them enough energy and enough protein. Very few people are under-nourished. On the other hand, many people eat too much food. In September, 1985, the National Advisory Council on Nutrition Education (NACNE) published a report which caused quite a stir. This NACNE report set out the results of a careful study of the diet of the average person in the UK. The NACNE report states that the diet of the **average** person in the UK includes

- too much fat, especially saturated fat (see p. 5) (Average intake should be reduced from 128 g/day to 101 g/day.)

- too much sugar
  (Average intake should be reduced from 104 g/day to 55 g/day.)
- too much salt
- too much alcohol
- not enough dietary fibre
  (Average intake should be increased from 20 g/day to 30 g/day.)
- not enough vitamins and minerals.

Some people eat in moderation. If the *average* consumption of fat, sugar, salt and alcohol is too high, other people must be consuming vast quantities. Some people eat plenty of cereals and vegetables. If the *average* consumption of dietary fibre, vitamins and minerals is low, some people must be eating a very poor diet.

### What are the results of the 'Western diet'?

Research workers have been trying to find out why people become ill. Their evidence shows that the fundamental causes of disease are

- smoking
- drinking too much alcohol
- lack of regular exercise
- stress and frustration
- eating the wrong food.

Diet is not the only cause of illness in rich countries, but an unhealthy diet is thought to cause

- obesity (overweight)
- constipation, which may lead to diseases of the intestines
- death from heart disease(the UK has one of the highest rates of death from heart disease in the world, 150 000 per year)
- diabetes.

### Obesity

Obesity is the build-up of an excessive amount of fat in the body. A fat person has to carry extra weight. This puts a strain on the heart and lungs, which have to work harder to move the body around. The obese person therefore tires more easily and is more likely to suffer from heart failure.

### Constipation

The dietary fibre in food is not digested. By adding bulk to the faeces, it helps to prevent constipation (see p. 2). On a

'Western diet', many people eat processed foods from which fibre has been removed (see Table 2.7, p. 26). They produce about 100 g of faeces daily. People who eat a diet of cereals and vegetables with a high fibre content produce 300–500 g of faeces daily. With a high fibre diet, it takes about 30 hours for food to pass through the gut; on low fibre diets, it may take 70 hours for food to pass through the gut.

These foods contain dietary fibre

The **appendix** is a small sack leading off from the alimentary canal. If it becomes infected, it has to be removed by surgery. Often appendicitis (infection of the appendix) is caused by a small hard lump of faeces blocking the appendix. Fibre in the diet (roughage) softens the faeces and also keeps them moving.

**Cancer of the colon** (bowel cancer) is the second commonest cause of death from cancer. (Lung cancer is the most common.) Cancer of the colon (bowel) is much more common among people on a low-fibre diet than among people on a high-fibre diet. Many scientists believe that *carcinogens* (cancer-producing substances) are made by bacteria in the colon. By making the faeces move faster through the colon, a high fibre content shortens the time for which the carcinogens are in contact with the colon.

## Diabetes

A person who is diabetic is unable to control the concentration of sugar in his or her blood. With too much sugar in the blood, the person feels sleepy; with too little sugar in the blood, the diabetic may pass into a coma and may die. Some people are more likely than others to develop diabetes because of their genes. Many medical research workers believe that diabetes is not entirely a matter of genes and say that a long period of eating too much sugary food will trigger the disease.

## Thrombosis and heart disease

As people grow older, their arteries become less elastic. If the lining of an artery becomes thickened with fat cells, the artery becomes narrower. It is then more difficult for blood to flow through the artery (see below). The blood pressure rises as blood is forced through narrow arteries. If a blood clot forms, it may be trapped by the fatty material and block the artery. The part of the body which receives blood from that artery is now deprived of blood. A blockage in an artery which supplies blood to the heart is called a **coronary thrombosis** and causes a **heart attack**; a blockage in an artery which supplies the brain is called a **cerebral thrombosis** and causes a **stroke**.

(a)                          (b)

(a) Cross section through a healthy artery

(b) In this artery, a fatty deposit restricts the flow of blood.

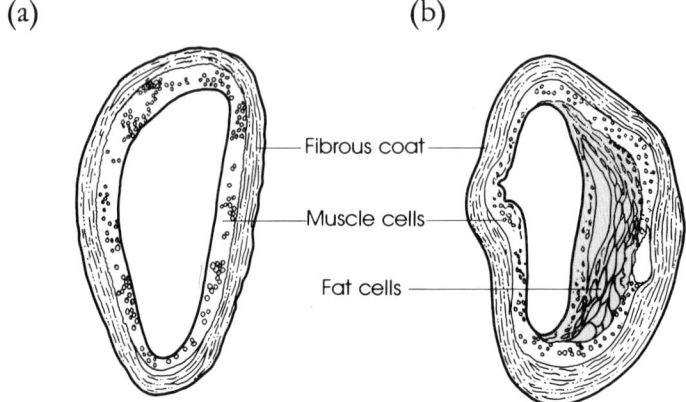

Fibrous coat

Muscle cells

Fat cells

The fatty deposits in the arteries contain large amounts of a substance called **cholesterol**. Everyone has cholesterol in their blood, but the amounts detected in the victims of heart disease are usually much greater than normal. Does eating fat increase the level of cholesterol in the blood? Many researchers believe that it does, especially if the fat is **saturated fat** (see p. 5). They believe that we should cut down the amount of saturated fat in our diet and replace it with **polyunsaturated fats** (see p. 6).

## What is the evidence that diet is to blame?

- The countries which have a high rate of heart disease are countries which consume a lot of dairy products and meat. When the consumption of fats and sugars in a country increases, the occurrence of heart diseases increases.
- When people from outside the West move to Western societies, they begin to suffer from 'Western' diseases. A

group of Japanese immigrants to the USA was studied. They contracted many more cases of heart disease than the same number of Japanese people living in Japan. When the immigrants started eating a 'Western diet', they became as likely to develop heart disease as native North Americans are.

- A 10 year study was made of 3000 American men. The men were put on a low-fat diet. Their cholesterol levels fell, and the number of heart attacks was less than expected for the age group.

## Does everyone agree?

The title of a report published in September, 1985, by the Joint Advisory Committee on Nutrition Education is 'Eating for a healthier heart'. It recommends that many people reduce their consumption of dairy foods (milk and milk products such as cheese and butter) as a means of cutting down heart disease. The Ministry of Agriculture, Fisheries and Food has difficulty in accepting the theory that the average person's intake of meat, cheese, eggs and milk should be cut down. Doctors are divided on the issue. Some doctors believe that the solution to the problem of heart disease lies in a low-fat diet; others do not. With 150 000 deaths from heart disease every year in the UK, those who believe in the theory want to see national changes in diet. Another Government committee, the Committee on Medical Aspects of Food, has said that the theory that heart disease is linked to diet is not proved.

## What do you do if you believe that the theory may well be correct?

Without being certain, many people accept the theory linking heart disease to diet. They are sufficiently convinced to take action. If you believe that a diet high in saturated fat and sugar is bad for you, what do you do?

*How can you cut down on saturated fat?*

| Cut down on: | Switch to: |
|---|---|
| Fried foods | Grilled or baked foods |
| High-fat cheeses | Cottage cheese |
| Whole milk | Skimmed or semi-skimmed milk |
| Cream | Low-fat yoghurt |
| Butter and hard margarine | Soft margarine |
| Fatty meats | Lean meat, poultry, fish |

*How can you cut down on sugar?*

| Cut down on: | Switch to: |
| --- | --- |
| White bread, cakes, biscuits | Wholemeal bread |
| Sweets | Fresh fruit |
| Sweetened canned fruit | Canned fruit in natural juices |

## A SLIMMING DIET

Whether you put on weight easily depends on genetics. Some people 'burn off' their excess food as energy and others quickly turn excess food into fat. Everyone can avoid putting on too much weight by controlling their diet. If you are on a 'slimming diet' because you want to lose weight, you should:

- Avoid sugar and processed foods with a high sugar content, e.g. sweets, cakes, biscuits and sweetened soft drinks.
- Eat more fruit, vegetables and wholemeal bread: their fibre content will make you feel full and prevent you from overeating.

## A VEGETARIAN DIET

**Vegetarians** do not eat fish or meat. They eat foods derived from plants: vegetables, fruits, cereals and nuts. Most vegetarians drink milk and eat eggs and milk products, e.g. cheese. Some vegetarians are **vegans**: they eat only foods derived from plants, and do not eat eggs, milk or milk products. **Omnivores** eat both plant and animal products.

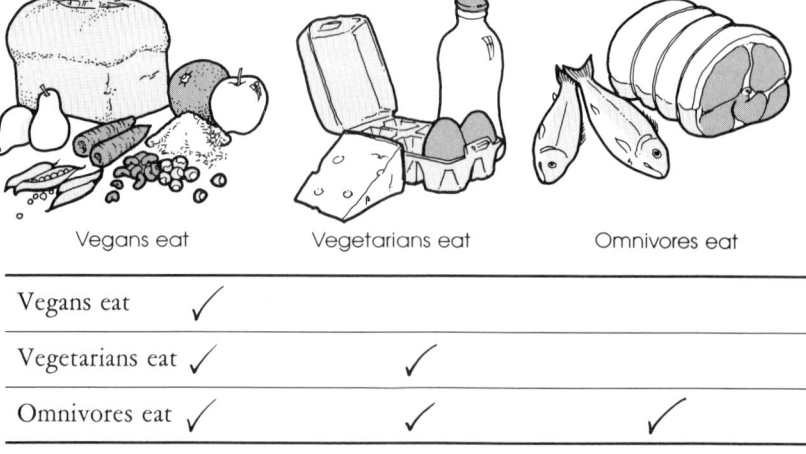

| | Vegans eat | Vegetarians eat | Omnivores eat |
| --- | --- | --- | --- |
| Vegans eat | ✓ | | |
| Vegetarians eat | ✓ | ✓ | |
| Omnivores eat | ✓ | ✓ | ✓ |

### Why do people become vegetarians?

**Religion**   Some religions do not allow killing animals. Hindus regard cows and bulls as sacred and never kill them,

Diets

no matter how old and useless they become. Some Hindus believe that we should never kill any animal. Buddhists have a rule that nobody may earn his living by taking life so no Buddhist could work as a fisherman or slaughterman. Muslims are forbidden by their religion to eat pork.

**Cruelty**   Many vegetarians do not like to think that animals have been killed or ill-treated to provide them with food. Intensive farming methods keep chickens in 'batteries': rows of tiny boxes in which the chickens cannot move around. They keep calves and pigs penned up instead of allowing them to wander round in a field (see below). These intensively reared animals never enjoy a normal life: they are treated as machines for converting plant foods into animal protein and fat. If they are prevented from walking about, they do not use as much energy, and soon become big enough for slaughter.

Free range pigs

Battery pigs

**Efficiency**   Cattle are able to obtain enough food by grazing poor ground which is too infertile for growing grain. Where grain is plentiful, however, cattle are often fattened on a diet of grain. They are reared in feedlots, large pens in which cattle can get all the grain and water they want without walking far. In the USA, 85% of the grain produced is fed to cattle. It takes 16 kg of plant protein to produce 1 kg of animal protein. This is wasteful: more people could obtain nourishment by eating the grain than by eating the beef which is the end-product.

Is using land to raise cattle a responsible thing to do when so many of the world's people are underfed and undernourished? For how many days will the produce from one hectare of land feed one person? That depends on which crop you grow!

Table 2.3 is taken from *The Real Cost* by Richard North (Chatto and Windus, 1986).

Table 2.3   **Protein value of some crops**

| Crop | Number of days supply of protein which 1 hectare of land will provide when this crop is grown |
|---|---|
| Soybeans | 5500 |
| Wheat | 2200 |
| Corn | 880 |
| Used as grazing for beef cattle | 190 |

**A slim figure**   Vegetarians generally eat less fat than omnivores. As a result, on average, vegetarians are slimmer than omnivores. In August, 1987, the pop-star Madonna announced that she had lost weight and gained fitness on a vegan diet. She is careful to eat a variety of vegan foods.
**A high fibre diet**   There is no fibre in meat. Vegetables, cereals and fruits provide the fibre in the diet (see pp. 16, 26).

**Disadvantages**   Vegetarians, especially vegans, have to be careful to get all the nutrients they need (see Table 2.4). Vitamin D may be missing from their diet, but the body can manufacture vitamin D in sunlight. The vitamin B12 in the diet may need to be supplemented. Some micro-organisms manufacture vitamin B12, and vegans can add to their food an extract of micro-organisms, e.g. Barmene, which contains the vitamin.

Table 2.4   **Sources of essential nutrients**

|  | Protein | Carbohydrate | Fats and oils | Vitamins B12 | C | D | Minerals Iron | Calcium |
|---|---|---|---|---|---|---|---|---|
| Animal products | Meat Fish Milk Eggs | | Meat Butter Cheese | Meat Cheese Eggs | Liver | Liver Fish oil Cheese Eggs | Meat Eggs | Milk Eggs Cheese Meat Fish |
| Plant products | Nuts Beans Cereals Seeds | Cereals Beans Fruit Potatoes | Margarine Nuts | Yeast extract Soya beans | Fruit Vegetables | Vegetable Margarine | Beans Green vegetables | Green vegetables Potatoes |

1) Draw a poster to illustrate one of the following:
   (a) Sugar is bad for you.
   (b) You need a good breakfast.

2) Draw a poster to show *either* what protein foods are *or* what kind of food a growing child needs.

3) Plan these meals:
   (a) a good breakfast (Explain your choice.)
   (b) a midday meal which is high in energy and fibre but low in fat
   (c) an evening meal which is high in energy and protein and contains minerals and vitamins.

4) Your head-teacher is worried about the badly balanced diet of some of the 14–16 year-olds in the school. The head wants to put up posters in the school cafeteria to help pupils with their choice of food.

   Design a poster which will give them some practical advice.

## Compare the quantities of energy supplied by different foods

You can find instructions in a text book and in Extending Science 7: *Energy* by J J Wellington (ST(P)).

# QUESTIONS ON CHAPTER 2

**1** If a 200 kg (14 stone) man needs to eat 120 g of protein a day, does a 14 year-old boy of 100 kg weight need to eat 60 g of protein a day? Explain your answer.

**2** According to the 1983 report of the National Advisory Council on Nutrition Education (NACNE), what is wrong with the diet of the average Briton?

What do NACNE believe to be the results of eating an unhealthy diet?

**3** What does 'obese' mean?
What is wrong with being obese?
What is the cure for obesity?

**4** What is 'dietary fibre'?
Explain the connection between dietary fibre and constipation.

**5** What is the name for a blockage in an artery?
What causes such a blockage?
What is the result?
How is a person's diet thought to affect their chances of blocked arteries?

**6** Imagine that your friend Flossie wants to lose weight. She speaks of going on a crash diet.
  (a) Explain what nutrients Flossie will lack if she cuts out milk, cheese and meat completely from her diet without substituting other foods.
  (b) Explain to her that a wiser course would be to substitute nutritious low-fat foods for high-fat foods.
  (c) Draw up a list of such low-fat foods for her.
  (d) What else should Flossie cut down on besides fat?
  (e) Advise her what changes she can make in her diet to cut down on this substance without losing nutritious foods.

**7** List the nutrients in milk
What essential nutrient is missing?
Why is milk a good diet for a baby but not for an adult?
What kind of milk is best for the very young baby?

**8** Refer to Table 2.4, p. 22.
  (a) What are the advantages to health of a vegetarian diet?
  (b) Certain nutrients may be lacking from a vegetarian diet. What are they?
  (c) How can vegetarians obtain these essential nutrients?

**9** My niece, Susan, who is twenty, wanted to lose a little weight. She heard that a friend had lost weight on a diet of baked beans and baked potatoes. Susan ate 500 g of baked beans and 1.00 kg of potatoes a day. Table 2.5 shows the constituents of Susan's food, and Table 2.6 shows her daily food requirement.

  (a) Explain why Susan lost weight.
  (b) Explain why she did not feel hungry.
  (c) Another friend warned her that she might be short of vitamin C. Was the friend right? Explain your answer.
  (d) Would Susan be short of any other vitamins?
  (e) What foods would you advise Susan to add to her diet?
  (f) Would you advise her to stay on this diet for a long time? Explain your answer.

Table 2.5  Percentage composition of some foods (from *Food Tables* by A E Bender and D A Bender, OUP, 1986)

| Food | Energy (kJ) | Protein (g) | Fat (g) | Carbo-hydrate (g) | Water (g) | Sodium (mg) | Calcium (mg) | Iron (mg) | Vitamin A (μg) | Vitamin B1 (mg) | Vitamin B2 (mg) | Vitamin C (mg) |
|---|---|---|---|---|---|---|---|---|---|---|---|---|
| Bananas | 330 | 1.0 | 0.3 | 20.0 | 70.0 | 0 | 0 | 0.4 | 200 | 0.04 | 0.07 | 10 |
| Beans (baked) | 270 | 5.0 | 0.5 | 10.0 | 74.0 | 480 | 45 | 1.4 | 0 | 0.07 | 0.05 | 0 |
| Bread (wholemeal) | 920 | 8.8 | 2.7 | 42.0 | 40.0 | 540 | 2.5 | 0 | 0 | 0.30 | 0.08 | 0 |
| Cheese (Cheddar) | 1670 | 26.0 | 34.0 | 0 | 37.0 | 600 | 800 | 0.4 | 400 | 0.04 | 0.50 | 0 |
| Fish (fried cod) | 710 | 21.0 | 8.0 | 4.0 | 65.0 | 180 | 110 | 1.2 | 0 | 0.10 | 0.10 | 0 |
| Milk (skimmed) | 140 | 3.4 | 0.1 | 5.0 | 91.0 | 50 | 130 | 0 | 0 | 0.04 | 0.20 | 1 |
| Potatoes (baked) | 360 | 2.0 | 0 | 20.0 | 58.0 | 0 | 0 | 0.06 | 0 | 0.10 | 0.03 | 10 |
| Potatoes (chips) | 1050 | 4.0 | 11.0 | 37.0 | 47.0 | 0 | 0 | 0.9 | 0 | 0.10 | 0.04 | 10 |

Table 2.6  Recommended daily amounts of nutrients (from *Food Tables* by A E Bender and D A Bender, OUP, 1986)

| | Energy (kJ) | Protein (g) | Calcium (mg) | Iron (mg) | Vitamin A (μg) | Vitamin B1 (mg) | Vitamin B2 (mg) | Vitamin C (mg) |
|---|---|---|---|---|---|---|---|---|
| Girl 3–4 | 1500 | 37 | 600 | 8 | 300 | 0.6 | 0.8 | 20 |
| Girl 7–8 | 8000 | 47 | 600 | 10 | 400 | 0.8 | 1.0 | 20 |
| Girl 12–14 | 9000 | 53 | 700 | 12 | 725 | 0.9 | 1.4 | 25 |
| Woman 18–54 | 9500 | 54 | 500 | 12 | 750 | 0.9 | 1.3 | 30 |
| Boy 12–14 | 11 000 | 66 | 700 | 12 | 725 | 1.1 | 1.4 | 25 |
| Man 18–34 (sedentary) | 10 500 | 63 | 500 | 10 | 750 | 1.0 | 1.6 | 30 |
| Man 18–34 (very active) | 14 000 | 84 | 500 | 10 | 750 | 1.3 | 1.6 | 30 |

**10** Angela, who is eighteen, went on a slimming diet of bananas and milk. She ate 1.5 kg of bananas and drank 1.0 kg of skimmed milk a day.

(a) Refer to Table 2.5. Calculate Angela's daily intake of energy, protein, fats, calcium, iron and vitamins A, B1, B2 and C.

(b) Compare the figures you obtained in (a) with those in Table 2.6.

(c) Say what nutrients Angela's diet lacks. What should she eat to make up for these shortages?

(d) What would be a better way of reducing weight?

**11** According to the NACNE report, we should aim to eat 30 g of fibre a day. Table 2.7 gives some figures for the fibre content of different foods.

Table 2.7   Fibre content of food (from *Food Tables* by A E Bender and D A Bender, OUP, 1986)

| Food | Dietary fibre in g per 100 g of food | Food | Dietary fibre in g per 100 g of food |
|---|---|---|---|
| Avocado pear | 2 | Flour, white | 4 |
| Beans, butter, boiled | 5 | Flour, wholemeal | 10 |
| Beef | 0 | Milk | 0 |
| Bread, white | 4 | Potatoes | 2 |
| Bread, wholemeal | 9 | Rice Krispies | 6 |
| Cabbage, boiled | 2 | Rice, white, raw | 3 |
| Carrots | 3 | Tomatoes, fried | 3 |
| Cheese | 0 | Weetabix | 9 |
| Fish | 0 | | |

On a certain day, Brenda and Tammy keep a careful record of what they eat (as shown in Table 2.8).

Table 2.8   **Brenda and Tammy**

| Brenda | Tammy |
|---|---|
| 50 g Rice Krispies | 50 g Weetabix |
| 250 g milk | 250 g milk |
| 200 g white bread | 200 g wholemeal bread |
| 50 g tomatoes | 50 g cheese |
| 100 g potatoes | 150 g potatoes |
| 100 g boiled cabbage | 100 g carrots |
| 150 g beef | 50 g boiled butter beans |
| 100 g avocado pear | 200 g fish |

(a) Calculate how much fibre each girl has eaten. Say whether it is more or less than the recommended daily amount.

(b) Say what else is important in a diet besides its fibre content.

**12** Calculate the energy, protein and iron provided by the following snacks.
*Bread and cheese:* 60 g wholemeal bread and 30 g cheese
*Fish and chips:* 150 g fried fish and 100 g chips.
You will need to use Table 2.5.

**13** The average 8-year old boy needs 49 g of protein a day. Calculate the cost of supplying him with 50 g of protein from each of the foods listed in the table below.

Table 2.9   **Some protein foods**

| Food | Protein (percentage) | Price of 1 kg | Cost of 50 g of protein |
|---|---|---|---|
| Baked beans | 5.0 | _____ | _____ |
| Beef steak | 19.0 | _____ | _____ |
| Fish fingers | 13.0 | _____ | _____ |
| Minced beef | 19.0 | _____ | _____ |
| Potatoes (baked) | 2.0 | _____ | _____ |
| White bread | 7.8 | _____ | _____ |
| Wholemeal bread | 8.8 | _____ | _____ |

(a) Make a copy of the table.
(b) Visit the shops and fill in the food prices.
(c) From the price of each food and its percentage of protein, calculate the cost of 50 g of protein from each food.
*Sample calculation*   If leg of lamb costs £2.00/kg and contains 18% protein, what is the cost of 50 g of protein from leg of lamb?

The cost of 50 g of leg of lamb is £2.00 $\times \dfrac{50}{1000}$

$$= £0.10$$

The cost of 50 g of protein is £0.10 $\times \dfrac{100}{18} = £0.56$

Enter your results in the table.

**14** A man aged 40 in a sedentary job needs about 10 000 kJ of energy a day. Assume that he takes about 4000 kJ in his evening meal. In this exercise, you are asked to find out how much it would cost him to obtain his energy requirement from packaged foods. If you do not have many packaged foods in your home, share the exercise between a group of pupils.

(a) Examine the labels of as many packaged foods as you can. You will see the energy content listed on the label and the price marked on the can or packet. Make a table of the food items you have found, as overleaf.

Table 2.10  **Some packaged foods**

| Food item | Energy content of packet (kJ) | Price of packet (£) | Cost of 4000 kJ (£/kJ) |
|---|---|---|---|
| Pot Noodle | 1297 | 0.49 | ———— |
| Beanfeast | 350 | 0.54 | ———— |

(b) Calculate the cost of obtaining 4000 kJ of energy from each of the different foods. For example,

Pot Noodle: Energy $=$ 1297 kJ, Price $=$ 49 p

$$\text{Cost of 4000 kJ energy} = 49 \times \frac{4000}{1297} \text{ p} = 151 \text{ p}$$
$$= £1.51$$

Enter the results of your calculations in your table.

(c) What is the most expensive source of energy in your table?

What is the least expensive source of energy in your table?

Do you think packaged foods are an economic source of energy?

(d) Why is it better to obtain energy from a number of different foods?

# WHY DOES FOOD SPOIL?

On 25 August, 1987, the *Daily Telegraph* carried this story:

### 'Church link as woman dies of bug'

'A 77-year-old spinster died of food poisoning and 73 other guests became ill after attending a vicar's garden party.

Environmental health officers have launched an investigation following the death of Miss Rita Jenner at Basingstoke district hospital on Saturday. They suspect that meat served at the party in Hampshire on August 9 might have been infected with *Salmonella*.

Seventy-five guests tucked into the chicken, ham, bacon and salami at the annual buffet. All but two of them were affected.'

## WHY DOES FOOD GO BAD AND WHY DOES BAD FOOD CAUSE FOOD POISONING?

The World Health Organisation estimates that 20% of the world's food is lost through spoilage. There are a number of causes:

- oxidation by air of fats and oils to produce rancid substances
- drying up as water evaporates from the surface
- the action of enzymes present in the food
- attack by micro-organisms (microbes) in the environment.

### Microbial spoilage

After animals are killed and fruits and vegetables are gathered, some of their cell walls break down. The nutrients which flow out of the cells are easier for micro-organisms (microbes) to feed on than they were in the living material. So micro-organisms can attack food better than they can attack living plants and animals. Bacteria, moulds and yeasts are the micro-organisms which bring about spoilage. The air contains many of them, and when they come into contact with food they grow and multiply. The food soon begins to look unappetising.

**Bacteria** are very tiny: one million bacteria weigh only about one millionth of one gram. Under the right conditions, bacteria multiply fast. When the number of bacteria reaches ten million per gram of food, the food looks obviously spoiled. Most bacteria grow better in neutral conditions. Some bacteria need oxygen; these are called **aerobic** bacteria. Some bacteria will grow only in the absence of oxygen; these are called **anaerobic** bacteria. Some bacteria can grow under both aerobic and anaerobic conditions. Bacteria are killed at 100 °C, but some produce spores which are heat-resistant.

A **spore** is a **dormant** state of a micro-organism. The life processes have been shut down to the minimum needed to keep the organism alive. Spores form when conditions are too harsh for normal growth. When better conditions return, the spores become active again and multiply. Spores can be carried long distances by air currents and in this way infect food.

Moist, warm food provides good growing conditions for micro-organisms. As micro-organisms grow, they produce waste products. Some bacteria are harmless: cheese and yoghurt are produced by bacterial action (see pp. 64–5). Some bacteria produce waste products which are toxic (poisonous) to animals. If people eat contaminated food, they are likely to suffer from **food poisoning**. The symptoms are called *intestinal upset* or *gastroenteritis* (sickness and diarrhoea). The common bacteria which cause food poisoning are *Salmonella*, *Staphylococcus* and *Clostridium*.

*The Independent* of 27 August, 1987 carried a report on food poisoning. Part of the report is shown on the next page.

Stilton cheese ripens through the action of harmless bacteria

### 'Salmonella cases increase sharply'

'Food poisoning caused by *Salmonella* has reached epidemic proportions and is costing millions of pounds in lost working hours and medical treatment, according to a leading public health official.

Latest statistics show the number of *Salmonella* cases in England and Wales is rising by about 25 per cent a year, and scientists expect it to continue doing so.

Dr Bernard Rowe, of the Public Health Laboratory Service which monitors outbreaks of food poisoning, said: "If you take into account lost earnings, medical costs and lost productivity, *Salmonella* is costing the country millions of pounds." '

*Salmonella* can be present in food without making the food look obviously bad. The bacterium produces a toxin *after* the infected food has been eaten. *Salmonella* does not form spores. It can be destroyed by heating at 60 °C for 15–20 minutes. *Salmonella* cannot multiply in a closed container (can or bottle), and it cannot multiply if food is kept cold. The danger arises if cooked food is allowed to remain at room temperature for several hours; these conditions are ideal for the growth of *Salmonella*.

*Salmonella* is one of the typhoid bacteria. It thrives inside people. Some people are *carriers* of typhus: although they are infected, they show no symptoms. If these people handle food which is kept under unhygienic conditions, the food will become infected and the disease will spread.

*Staphylococcus* causes pimples, boils and septic wounds. It also causes food poisoning, so people who have septic cuts on their hands should not handle food. A bandage or plaster over a septic cut is no protection because once a bandage or plaster becomes wet it does not stop germs from reaching the food. *Staphylococcus* produces a toxin after the infected food has been eaten. It does not form spores, and it is quickly destroyed by boiling. Foods which are not heated to such high temperatures, e.g. cream-filled pastries, are the source of food poisoning from *Staphylococcus*.

The most dangerous type of food poisoning is caused by *Clostridium botulinum*. This micro-organism is present in soil and contaminates vegetables. It is present in the intestines of animals and infected people. A person who has been working in the fields or handling manure can spread the bacterium to food. The toxin produced by this bacterium is called *botulin*. It causes food poisoning called *botulism*, which results in paralysis and even death. Botulin is one of the most toxic of substances. Someone has calculated that 400 g would be enough to kill the entire world population. The toxin is destroyed by heating, but the microbe itself can withstand high temperatures. *Clostridium* is especially dangerous because it can form spores. The spores are destroyed by heating food at 121 °C for 10 minutes. Food which has been improperly bottled or canned may contain *Clostridium*. This will live in the canned food, producing botulin, and the toxin will cause food poisoning when the contents of the can are eaten. Commercial canning and bottling plants employ conditions which will kill *Clostridium*.

**Moulds** are fungi. They are microscopic plants which have no chlorophyll. Moulds need oxygen. This is why they are found on the surface of foods such as cheese and jam. Bread is soon attacked by moulds because its porous structure allows air to get inside it. Moulds will not grow in strongly acidic solutions: you will not find a jar of pickles going mouldy. Moulds can grow slowly inside a home refrigerator. Heat treatment kills moulds, but their spores are difficult to kill: sterilisation above 100 °C is needed.

**Yeasts** are fungi. The powdery substance you can see on the skins of grapes and plums is a yeast. Yeasts also occur in soil. Yeasts can withstand acidic conditions, high concentrations of salt and sugar and the absence of oxygen. Yeasts and yeast spores are easily killed by heating to 100 °C. Many yeasts are useful. Yeasts are used in the production of alcohol and bread (see pp. 46, 57).

Food which has been attacked by micro-organisms may look or smell unappetising. In many cases, however, contaminated food may still look good. This is dangerous because a food which seems good is much more likely to cause food poisoning than one which is so obviously bad that no-one is tempted to eat it.

## HOW CAN YOU AVOID FOOD POISONING?

To preserve food and avoid food poisoning, you need to eliminate one of the conditions which micro-organisms need for growth. These are

- nutrients
- moisture
- a favourable temperature (neither too high nor too low)
- time (Under optimum conditions, many bacteria can divide once every 20 minutes. If division continues at this rate, a

single micro-organism could produce 2 million offspring within 7 hours. In practice, the growth rate slows down as the colony of bacteria runs out of food.)

- air (Moulds and some bacteria are *aerobic*: they need air. Other bacteria are *anaerobic*: they do not need air. Yeasts can grow either aerobically or anaerobically.)
- a favourable pH (Most micro-organisms prefer neutral conditions.)

## QUESTIONS ON CHAPTER 3

**1** What types of micro-organisms attack food?
Why are they more able to attack food than living plants and animals?

**2**

A meat counter at a Sainsbury supermarket

    (a) What precautions have been taken in the supermarket shown above to protect meat from attack by (i) bacteria and (ii) flies?
    (b) What kind of warehouse should be used to store meat before it reaches the supermarket?

**3** Why are you more likely to get mould on the surface of jam than in the interior?
Why does bread go mouldy inside as well as on the surface?
Why does pickled beetroot not go mouldy?

**4** If you were the manager of a supermarket, what steps would you take to ensure that your customers do not suffer from food poisoning?

**5** Name a micro-organism which causes food poisoning and is sometimes present in cooked meats. What precautions will avoid the growth of this micro-organism?

**6** Imagine that you are the manager of a restaurant. You have taken on new staff in the kitchen. List three instructions which you would give them about handling food in a hygienic manner.

**7** Why are people more likely to develop food poisoning from eating meat and fish than from eating fruit and vegetables?

**8** What is the most dangerous kind of food poisoning? Name the micro-organism which causes this type of food poisoning.
Explain how it can infect food.
How can the micro-organism be destroyed?

**9** The table shows figures published by the Institution of Environmental Health Officers.

Table 3.1  **Cases of food poisoning**

| Year | Food poisoning cases in England and Wales |
|------|-------------------------------------------|
| 1973 | 8 574 |
| 1975 | 11 943 |
| 1977 | 9 204 |
| 1979 | 11 881 |
| 1981 | 10 665 |
| 1982 | 12 684 |
| 1983 | 15 168 |

    (a) How big is the increase in food poisoning between 1973 and 1983?
    (b) Which two-year period shows the biggest increase?
    (c) Suggest reasons which may explain the increase in food poisoning.
    (d) Suggest precautions which should be taken to reduce the occurrence of food poisoning (i) in the home, (ii) in restaurants.

# WORDSQUARE

Trace or photocopy the wordsquare (see note on p. ii).
Solve the clues, and ring the twenty words. Answers can read
from left to right, from right to left, upwards, downwards
or diagonally.

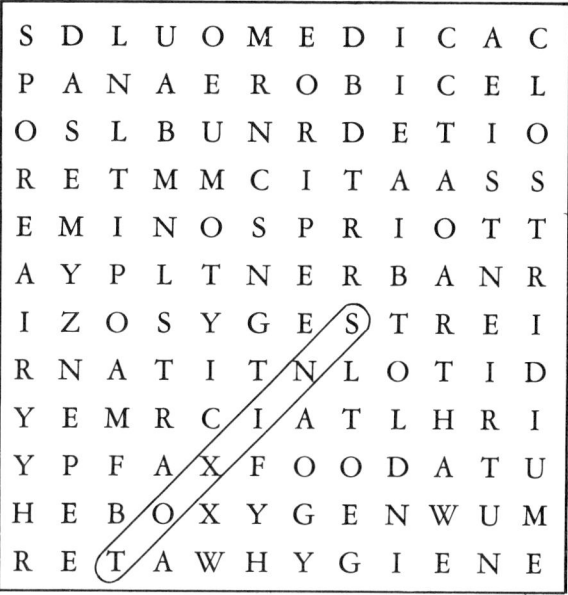

1  Poisons produced by
   bacteria (6)
2  They help chemical reactions
   to take place in plants and
   animals (7)
3, 4, 5,  Three types of micro-
   organisms which attack
   food (8, 6, 6)
6  Dormant state of micro-
   organism (5)
7  Moulds need this (6)
8  A group of bacteria (6)
9  This type of bacterium does
   not need air (9)
10, 11  Two micro-organisms
   which cause serious food
   poisoning (10, 11)
12, 13  Needed by all micro-
   organisms (5, 9)

14  Needed by some micro-
    organisms (3)
15  This chemical condition must
    be right for micro-organisms
    to grow (2)
16  Moulds cannot grow under
    these conditions (4)
17  Do this with meat to slow
    down the growth of micro-
    organisms (11)
18  Do this with frozen foods
    before cooking (4)
19  The kind of fruit that attracts
    flies (4)
20  This must be good in food
    shops to prevent food
    poisoning (7)

# 4 METHODS OF PRESERVING FOOD

Modern food processing methods can preserve food for long periods of time. To keep food wholesome, the growth of micro-organisms must be prevented. Some preserving methods are **bacteriocidal**: they kill all the micro-organisms. They do this either by eliminating one of the conditions needed for growth (p. 32–3) or by using chemicals to kill the microbes. Other methods are **bacteriostatic**: they reduce the activity of micro-organisms to a low level without actually killing them.

## REMOVAL OF WATER

Foods which contain plenty of water can easily be used as food by micro-organisms. A number of techniques are used for removing some of the water in a food. It is not necessary to remove *all* the water to stop bacteria, yeasts and moulds growing on food.

### Air drying

This is one of the oldest methods of food preservation. Fish can be gutted and then hung up in the sun and wind to dry. Vegetables, e.g. peas and beans, and fruits, e.g. dates and figs, can be spread out on racks to dry. Dried foods are easy to store and can be kept for long periods. When they are placed in water, they absorb liquid, swell up to their actual size, and can then be eaten.

Modern methods of air drying are:

- Roller drying. The food (e.g. potato flakes) is passed over heated rollers.
- Tunnel drying. The food moves on a conveyor belt through a warm tunnel.
- Fluidised bed drying. The food (e.g. vegetables) is chopped up and put into a column. Warm air blowing through the column from the bottom keeps the particles of food in motion.

### Vacuum drying

Water vaporises more quickly if the air pressure around it is below atmospheric pressure. This is the basis of **vacuum drying**. The method is used to make milk powder. Milk is sprayed into a heated space at reduced pressure. Water vaporises to leave a dry powder. This tastes better than milk which has been dried by boiling.

### Freeze drying

The food is frozen quickly and then warmed under reduced presure. The crystals of ice in the food *sublime* (turn from solid into vapour). Freeze-dried foods (e.g. instant coffee) contain practically no moisture. They can be stored at normal temperatures. Freeze-dried foods are often packed under nitrogen. If the container is filled with nitrogen and then sealed, dried foods will keep for two or three years.

Sealed under nitrogen

### The addition of salt or sugar

Salting is one of the oldest methods of preserving food. For over 100 years, fishermen have preserved their catches by packing them in salt. If a micro-organism is in contact with a concentrated solution, such as a salt or sugar solution, water passes out of the micro-organism through its cell membrane into the solution. As a result, the microbes become dehydrated and die. The salted or sweetened food is therefore preserved. (The flow of water through a membrane from a dilute solution into a more concentrated solution is called **osmosis**.)

### A few questions

1) Why does bacon, which is salted pork, keep well?

2) How does the high concentration of sugar in jam prevent it from going mouldy? Why does mould appear on the surface of the jam before it appears in the centre?

3) Why can sweetened condensed milk be kept for several weeks after the can is opened?

## FREEZING

Freezing is being used more and more for food preservation. It does not alter the taste of the food as do older methods such as salting. Now, deep sea trawlers have giant freezer compartments so that fish can be frozen soon after it is caught. Refrigerated ships carry meat thousands of miles from New Zealand to the UK At temperatures below 0 °C, bacteria and most moulds carry on their life processes very, very slowly. When frozen food is allowed to thaw, the bacteria and moulds become active again.

### Refrigeration

If food is stored at 0–5 °C, micro-organisms grow only slowly.

### Deep-freezing

Most fresh foods contain over 60% water. This water freezes below 0 °C because the substances dissolved in it lower its freezing point. At −5 °C, 64% of the water in peas is frozen; at −18 °C, 87% is frozen. If water is frozen, it cannot be used by microbes. This is why at −18 °C or below, food can be preserved for long periods. For top quality, food should be frozen quickly. In a **blast freezer**, a blast of very cold air is blown over a conveyor belt carrying the food.

### Frozen food

In food kept at −18 °C, microbes are inactive but not dead. You have to take care to cook the food thoroughly before it is eaten. If you do not do this, as food warms up the microbes multiply and soon reach harmful numbers.

When food is frozen, the water in it forms crystals of ice. As water freezes, it expands. The expanding ice-water causes a partial breakdown of the cell walls. When food is thawed, the cell contents can seep through the damaged cell walls. Micro-organisms attack the nutritious material. This is why thawed food will keep less well than fresh food.

## STERILISATION

Heating food to a high temperature kills micro-organisms and their spores. This process is called *sterilisation*. If the food is to be kept for long periods, it must be sterilised in a sealed container, e.g. a can or a bottle, which will prevent fresh micro-organisms from entering after the food has been sterilised. Almost any type of food can be canned or bottled. Some vegetables must first be *blanched* (heated to 90 °C) to kill enzymes on their skins. Some fruits are first mixed with sugar syrup.

Canned vegetables and meats are heated to 115 °C; fruits are heated to only 100 °C. They are more acidic than vegetables and meat, and this acidity protects them. The food is placed while still hot in cans. After the cans have been sealed, the contents cool and contract (see below).

Canned food (a) The reduction in pressure as the contents cool sucks in the ends of the can. (b) A bulge in a can means that gas has been formed by micro-organisms reproducing and respiring. The can is 'blown' and should be destroyed.

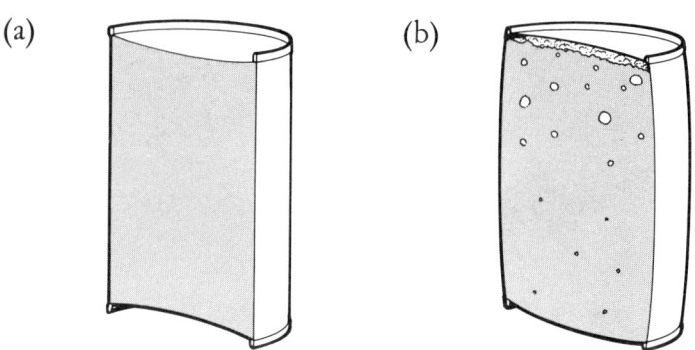

(a)    (b)

Cans are made of iron which has been plated with tin to protect the iron from rusting. Foods of high acidity, e.g. fruits, need a special 'lacquered can' so that the acid does not come into contact with tin.

The use of pressure cookers has made sterilisation methods much more efficient. Under a pressure greater than atmospheric pressure, water boils above 100 °C. The modern HTST (high temperature short time) technique employs a temperature of 121 °C for 3 minutes. These conditions are drastic enough to kill spores of *Clostridium botulinum*, which are particularly dangerous (see p. 32), and all other harmful organisms. It is difficult to be sure of obtaining the right conditions in the home, and preserving meat and fish is too risky for home preserving methods. Preserving fruit and vegetables is less risky because the acid they contain makes it more difficult for micro-organisms to survive.

## PASTEURISATION

**Pasteurisation** is partial sterilisation. The process was named after Louis Pasteur, the famous French scientist. The most important application of pasteurisation is in making cows' milk safe for human consumption (see p. 62). (see p. 62) Pasteurisation kills many but not all the bacteria in the milk. Fortunately, the harmful bacteria are killed. The usual treatment is 72 °C for 15 seconds. Pasteurisation does not alter the taste of milk. It enables milk to keep for several days if it is kept cool.

## PICKLING

If food is acidic, it will slow down the growth of micro-organisms. Vinegar (a solution of the weak acid, ethanoic acid) is used in pickling. Yoghurt keeps well because it contains lactic acid.

Pickles

## CURING

Meats, e.g. bacon, are soaked in or injected with a solution of salts. Sodium chloride, potassium nitrate and sodium nitrite are the salts used. They slow down the growth of microbes. Recently, people have started to worry about the use of nitrites. It is possible that nitrites could react with proteins to form nitrosoamines, which are *carcinogenic* (cancer-forming). The danger of food poisoning by *Salmonella* is, however, much greater than the danger from nitrites.

Staff inspecting bacon
before it is packaged

## SULPHUR DIOXIDE AND BENZOIC ACID

Sulphur dioxide and sulphites, benzoic acid and benzoates are used as preservatives.

Preserved by sulphur
dioxide and sulphites

Preserved by benzoic
acid and benzoates

# IRRADIATION

The American and Russian space crews on the Apollo-Soyuz mission in 1975 ate **irradiated** food. Radioactive elements give off particles and energy called **radiation**. Exposing things to radiation is called **irradiation**. Very small doses of radiation are sufficient to kill the micro-organisms that spoil food. The dose of radiation which the food receives is carefully calculated to be enough to sterilise it and insufficient to make it radioactive. Many countries irradiate food, but in the UK the irradiation of food is banned. The position may change, since in 1986 a scientific committee recommended that the Government allow the use of radiation for preserving food.

Symbol for irradiated food

ACTIVITIES

1) **Making jam**: Ask your Home Economics Department for a recipe.

2) **Blanching**
The colour changes which occur when some fruits and vegetables are cut and their surfaces are exposed to air are due to enzyme action. Plan an experiment to find out whether blanching (at 90 °C for 2 minutes) will prevent discolouration. You could use chipped potatoes and sliced peeled apples for your experiments.
Show your plan to your teacher, and if he or she approves, carry it out.

3) **Some methods of preservation**
A slice of apple turns brown if you leave it in the air. How can you stop this happening? Plan an experiment to compare the rate of browning of
(a) a slice of apple left in the air
(b) a slice of apple immersed in water
(c) a slice of apple immersed in a solution of sugar
(d) a slice of apple immersed in a solution of salt
(e) a slice of apple immersed in vinegar.
Which if these methods (if any) would you recommend for preserving apples?

## QUESTIONS ON CHAPTER 4

**1** How does food preservation benefit (a) the variety of our diets, (b) the housewife who works outside the home, (c) the price of food?

**2** Why is it easier to preserve fruit than to preserve vegetables?

**3** Explain the reasons why, when you make jam at home, you do the following:
(a) boil the fruit
(b) add sugar (two reasons)
(c) pour the jam into clean jars
(d) cover the jam jars with lids.

**4** Explain (a) why milk is pasteurised and (b) why pasteurised milk does not keep for long.

**5** Discuss the following question.
'Irradiating food to prolong its life is a help to manufacturers, exporters and retailers. Is it of benefit to the consumer?'

**6** Sort this list of preservation methods into two lists: List A – methods which alter the appearance and taste of food and List B – methods which retain the original character of the food.
Air drying  Dehydration  Canning  Pickling  Smoking Salting  Refrigeration  Fast freezing  Freeze drying Vacuum drying

**7** Look at the figure on p. 41. Why is the woman wearing rubber gloves? Why is she wearing a cap? What treatment has the bacon received to preserve it? What are the cylinders of nitrogen at the left-hand side of the picture used for?

# WORDPUZZLE: A DOZEN WAYS TO KEEP FOOD

Trace or photocopy the wordpuzzle (see note on p. ii), and then fill in the answers to the clues. Fill in the answers to the clues horizontally.

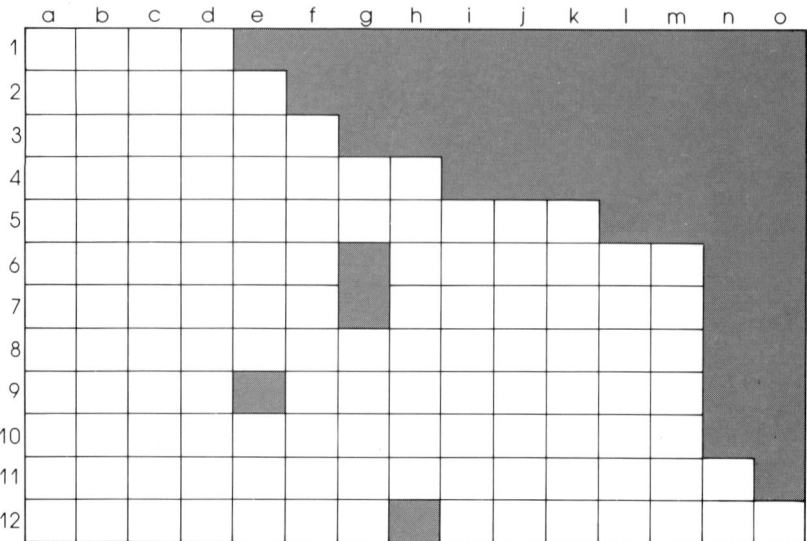

1 Adding this is an old way of keeping food (4)
2 This helps jam to keep (5)
3 Preserving meat by injecting salts (6)
4 Use this method to preserve beetroot and onions (8)
5 A modern method of preserving food which has not caught on widely (11)
6 Removal of water under reduced pressure (two words 6, 6)
7 Removal of water at low temperature (two words 6, 6)

8 You use this method at home to keep food (13)
9 A popular method of preserving food to retain its taste (two words 4, 8)
10 Heating food to kill all micro-organisms (13)
11 A method of preserving milk (14)
12 Chemical used as a preservative for dried fruits and vegetables (two words 7, 7)

Fill in the grid below with the correct letters selected from your answers. You will be able to read a message about food.

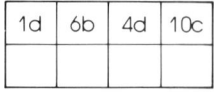
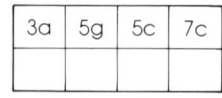

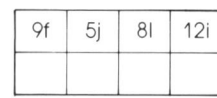
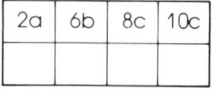

# 5

# BEER AND WINE

## 'SOVIET DRINKS PURGE BRINGS TALE OF EAU'

This article appeared in the *Daily Telegraph*, 11 August, 1987.

'A man who asked for eau de cologne after-shave in a Russian shop was refused by the assistant because she could sell it only after two o'clock. "But I need it for shaving," he persisted. "Then shave after two," she answered with steely logic.

The man's tale of eau, in yesterday's *Pravda*, highlighted a worrying aspect of Mr Gorbachev's brave attempt to change the heavy drinking habits of millions of Russians. The crackdown on drinking has raised the drinking age to 21, restricted the opening hours of liquor stores, cut the number of outlets and reduced the production of vodka.

But these measures have led to a large increase in the brewing of moonshine and an increase in the consumption of drink substitutes like window cleaning fluid, cockroach poison and cheap eau de cologne. There has been such a large rush for eau de cologne that some shops have run out of it and others have been forced to ration it. Women who wish to be fragrant have been angered to find that it has become difficult or impossible to find cheap brands of cologne.

Like Mr Arkady Grachev, who wrote to *Pravda* from the northern region of Murmansk because he wanted to put after-shave on his chin and not down his throat, people have been forced to buy the expensive perfumes that drunks cannot afford. Mr Grachev described himself as a sober fellow who was suffering because of the drinking habits of others.

Although a local official said the shop had misunderstood the rules, it seems the staff thought they were under instruction to restrict cologne sales until after 2 pm, in line with the new liquor store rules.'

## A few questions

1) Why do you think Mr Gorbachev wants Russians to drink less alcohol?

2) What has he done to reduce drinking?

3) Why do some people now want to drink eau de cologne?

4) What is eau de cologne normally used for?

5) What is 'moonshine'? How does it get its name?

6) Can you see a way out of the difficulty faced by users of eau de cologne?

Alcoholic drinks contain a compound called **ethanol**, which has the formula $C_2H_5OH$. It is a member of the family of compounds called **alcohols**. Ethanol is the most widely used member of the alcohol family, and people often refer to *ethanol* as *alcohol*. Ethanol is the only alcohol which is safe to drink, and ethanol can be drunk only in small quantities before it becomes harmful.

A model of a molecule of ethanol

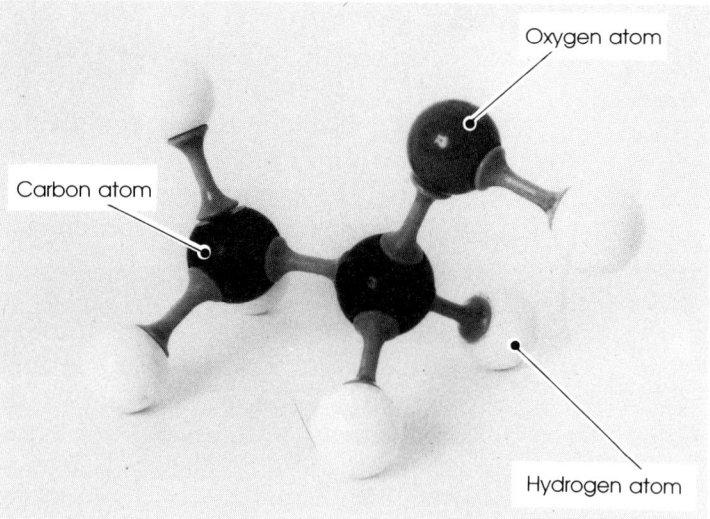

Both beer and wine contain ethanol. Both are made by using yeast to ferment the sugar called **glucose**. Yeasts are micro-organisms which feed on glucose and other nutrients with the formation of ethanol and carbon dioxide. The reaction is called **fermentation**:

$$\text{Glucose (a sugar)} \xrightarrow{\text{yeast}} \text{Ethanol (an alcohol)} + \text{Carbon dioxide}$$

Wine is the fermented juice of fruit, usually grapes. Beer is made from cereals. First, the starch in a cereal such as barley is converted into sucrose and then the sucrose is fermented.

# BEER MAKING

Barley is the chief grain crop used for the production of beer.

A plant operator checks the **wort** at an Ind Coope brewery

Beer contains 3–7% ethanol. The ethanol contents of some other drinks are: lager, 3–4%; ale, 6%; stout, 5–7%. When the can or bottle is opened, carbon dioxide comes out of solution, causing a foam to build up. In beer, the foam 'head' stays because beer contains proteins and unfermented carbohydrates which form a structure to support the foam. In carbonated soft drinks, the carbon dioxide comes out of solution as bubbles and escapes.

## A few questions

1) What are (a) malt and (b) yeasts?

2) What jobs are done by (a) malt enzymes and (b) yeast enzymes?

3) Why are hops added in beer making?

4) What use is made of *spent hops*?

5) How is it that the brewer both buys yeast and has a surplus of yeast to sell? Who does he sell it to?

6) Why is beer stored for a while before it is sold?

7) Why does beer need to be pasteurised?

8) Why does beer have a 'head'?

**ACTIVITIES**

## Making ginger beer

Ask your Home Economics department for a recipe.

# From barley to beer

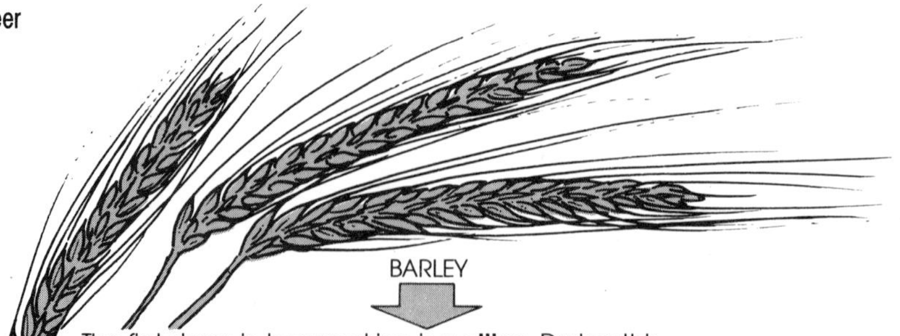

BARLEY

The first stage in beer-making is **malting**. During this stage, some of the starch breaks down and enzymes develop.
1) Barley kernels are kept damp and warm for a week. The grains of barley **germinate**, that is, the new plants start to grow.
2) The germinated barley is dried in a kiln at 70°C for 2 days. This stops growth and improves the flavour.

After this treatment, the barley is called **malt**.

Other starches, e.g. cornstarch, are added.

Water is added.

The mixture is **mashed**: crushed and cooked for 1–2 hours. Enzymes in the malt convert starches from the malt and the added starches into sugars.

**Spent grain** settles out. It is sold as cattle feed.

Hops are added. Their bitter flavour counters the sweetness of the sugars.

The sweet product of mashing is called **wort**. It is boiled for 2–3 hours in **coppers** and then filtered.

**Spent hops** are sold for use as fertiliser.

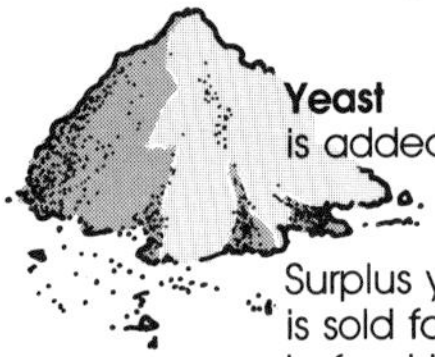

**Yeast** is added

The filtrate passes into a **fermentation tank**. where it is kept cool for a week.

Surplus yeast. is sold for use in food items.

During fermentation the wort is changed into beer. The yeast multiplies, and the brewer ends up with about five times as much yeast as he started with.

Beer is stored in barrels for 2–6 months. As solids settle, the beer clarifies. Slow chemical reactions take place with the production of flavourful compounds.

The beer is **pasteurised**. If it is to be sold in cans or bottles, it is filtered. Carbon dioxide is passed under pressure into the beer.

The beer is packed in cans, bottles or barrels.

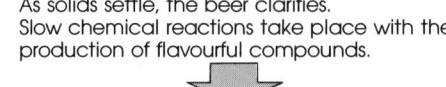

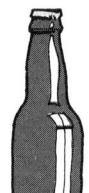

## WINE

**Wine** is fermented grape juice. The juice of other fruits may also be fermented but then it is described as, for example, peach wine or apple wine. You can often see a powdery substance growing on the skins of fruit, e.g. grapes and plums. This is a yeast. In wine making, grapes are crushed to produce a **must**. Then the enzymes which are present in the yeasts on the skins **ferment** the sugar content of the grapes. Ethanol (alcohol) and carbon dioxide are formed.

This 1878 wood engraving shows how wine was made a century ago

In a warm climate, grapes ripen fully and contain a high level of sugar. In a cooler climate, grapes will be less sweet. A low sugar level is corrected by the addition of sugar; this technique is called **fortification**. Each 1.00% of sugar ferments to give 0.55% of alcohol. The alcohol content of wine ranges from 9% to 14%. A minimum level of 9% is needed to kill micro-organisms. The fermentation of grapes is similar to that of barley. But *wild yeasts* (yeasts which are not needed for fermentation) grow on the skins of grapes. Sulphur dioxide and sulphites are used to kill off these wild yeasts. Fortunately, the wine yeasts on the skins are not harmed by sulphur dioxide. Wine yeasts can live in the high concentrations of alcohol found in wines. In time, they clump together and settle out so the wine does not taste of yeast. Sulphur dioxide also prevents oxidation of ethanol to ethanoic acid (the acid in vinegar). Producers do not want their wine to taste of vinegar!

### Different kinds of wine

The colour of red wines comes from pigments in the grape skins. White wines are made by fermenting grapes without their skins. Sparkling wines (bubbly wines) are produced by adding more sugar after fermentation has taken place and allowing the extra sugar to be fermented, with the formation of excess carbon dioxide. (This is dangerous for home wine-makers to attempt. They tend to add too much sugar so that too much carbon dioxide forms, and the bottles may explode.) Another way of making a sparkling wine is to add carbon dioxide from a cylinder of the gas.

## SPIRITS

Some people like drinks with a higher alcohol content than beer and wine. **Spirits**, such as gin, whisky, brandy and rum contain about 35% ethanol. They are made by distillation. After fermentation, the mash is heated to boiling and distilled. Ethanol is distilled over and collected.

The Lagavulin whisky distillery

### A few questions

1) What is the alcohol content of (a) beer, (b) wine, (c) whisky?

2) Why is sulphur dioxide added to wine?
   Why is carbon dioxide added to wine?
   What is the main difference between the method of making white wine and the method of making red wine?
   What do wine-makers mean by a 'good year'? What can they do to improve wine in a bad year?

## DRINKING ALCOHOL

Ethanol is described in medical terms as a **depressant**. This does not mean that it makes people feel depressed. By *depressing* (suppressing) feelings of fear and anxiety, small

One unit of alcohol

$\frac{1}{2}$ pint of beer or cider

1 glass of table wine

1 glass of sherry

1 measure of whisky/gin/rum/brandy

quantities of ethanol make people feel relaxed. Ethanol is completely soluble in water. When it is swallowed, it is absorbed through the stomach and intestines and passed into the blood stream. As the concentration of ethanol in the blood stream increases, it begins to affect the drinker. Alcohol is absorbed more slowly if the drinker has eaten a meal. You feel the effects of alcohol more on an empty stomach. Large people are less affected by alcohol than small people are. Men can tolerate more alcohol than women can. Alcohol is often measured in *units* (see the diagram above).

For an average 10 stone (64 kg) man, the effects of drinking alcohol are:

1 unit:      no obvious effect
2 units:    feeling more cheerful
3 units:    becoming very talkative
5 units:    increase in reaction times; blood alcohol probably above the legal level for driving
12 units: slurred speech, aggressive behaviour, loss of balance, blurred vision
24 units: unconsciousness

Alcohol has a *depressant* effect on the nerves which control muscles. Drinkers' speech becomes slurred, they walk unsteadily, and their reaction times become longer. This affects a drinker's ability to drive a car or a motorcycle. Drivers need to react quickly to other vehicles and to pedestrians; long reaction times make it dangerous to drive with a high level of alcohol in the blood. Alcohol is the largest single common factor in road accidents. A survey of 16–18 year-old drivers involved in road accidents showed that half of them had drunk too much. Every day 3 people are killed and 70 are injured in accidents involving drivers who have had too much to drink. At night, two-thirds of accidents are alcohol-related. Someone who has had a very long drinking session at night may still have more than the legal blood alcohol concentration when he drives to work in the morning (see the graph on the next page).

Drinking large amounts of alcohol regularly causes damage to the arteries, the liver, the kidneys and the brain. People who drink more than is good for their health are said to **abuse** alcohol. They do not *use* it properly, in moderation; they *misuse* it or *abuse* it. Many people drink so often that they find that they cannot manage without alcohol; they need to feel a little 'under the influence' all the time. They have become *alcoholics*. There are about 30 000 alcoholics in the UK. Frequent 'hangovers' after excessive drinking make a person do badly at his or her job. Bad temper and violent behaviour brought on by drinking have been responsible for the breakdown of many families, friendships and love affairs.

**How long does it last?**

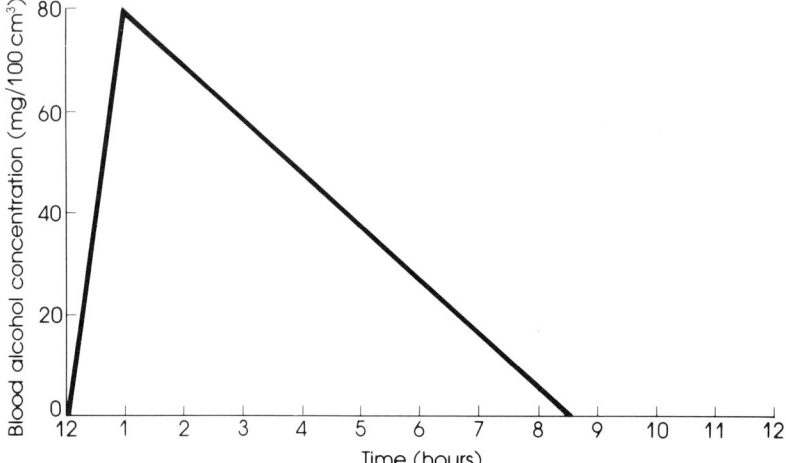

Methanol, $CH_3OH$, is a poisonous substance. Drinking only small amounts of methanol is very dangerous. Over a 3–4 hour period, drinking 10 cm³ of methanol may cause blindness, and 30 cm³ can cause death.

**ACTIVITIES**

1) Design a poster to show either 'Alcohol can be dangerous' or 'Don't drink and drive'.

2) Carry out a survey:
'Where were you when you had your first alcoholic drink?'
Ask the question of as many young people as you can. List their replies in a copy of the table. Then work out percentages and enter them in your table.

| Place | Number of boys | Number of girls | Percentage of boys | Percentage of girls |
|---|---|---|---|---|
| At home | | | | |
| At a friend's house | | | | |
| At a relation's house | | | | |
| At a party | | | | |
| In a pub | | | | |
| In a disco or club | | | | |
| Somewhere else | | | | |
| Non-drinker | | | | |

Construct a bar chart to show the percentages.

Can you see any differences in the patterns for boys and girls?

Is the percentage of non-drinkers the same for boys and girls?

Where did most of the people in your survey take their first alcoholic drink?

3)  The table below shows how the total amount of drink consumed by two age groups was divided between wine, spirits and beer.

| Men Age in years | Drinks consumed by this age group | | |
|---|---|---|---|
| | Wine | Spirits | Beer |
| 18–24 | 6% | 6% | 88% |
| over 55 | 12% | 22% | 66% |

(a) Draw a bar graph or a pie chart to illustrate the figures.

(b) Write a sentence or two summarising the difference between the tastes of the two groups.

(c) Conduct your own survey. Ask ten men in each of the age groups: 'Which alcoholic drink do you drink the most of?' Then ask ten women in each age group. Do the replies show any differences (i) between men and women, (ii) between young and old?

## QUESTIONS ON CHAPTER 5

**1** Copy and complete the passage.
Beer and wine contain an alcohol called _____. Industrial spirit is made unfit to drink by the addition of a poisonous alcohol called _____. Beer and wine are made by a chemical reaction called _____, in which a sugar called _____ is converted into the liquid _____ and the gas _____. This chemical reaction is brought about by _____, which is a living _____. The starting material for making wine is _____. Beer making starts with _____.

**2** Why do people laugh at a person who is drunk?

**3** Imagine that your friend Bob, who is 18, has a new motor scooter. After 2 hours in the pub, he invites his girl friend to ride on the back. Bob is a learner. Write a short story about what you would say to him and whether or not he takes your advice and what happens.

**4** You have gone to a party with a friend who is driving his parents' car. At the end of the evening, your friend has obviously had too much to drink, but he insists that he can drive. What do you do?

**5** Three people open a litre bottle of wine at 6 p.m. and finish the bottle between them by 9 p.m. Unknown to them, the wine had been adulterated with 3% of methanol.
   (a) Calculate the volume of methanol which each person has drunk (on average).
   (b) Are the people in any danger? Explain your answer.

**6** Why do the police advise 'Don't drink and drive'?

# BREAD

## BREAD MAKING

Like the production of beer and wine, bread making involves yeast enzymes. Yeast enzymes catalyse the fermentation of sugars to produce ethanol and carbon dioxide. In baking, it is carbon dioxide that is the important fermentation product because it makes bread and cakes rise. Different varieties of yeast are used in brewing and baking.

### Flour

Wheat grains are ground to produce flour. There are different varieties of wheat. In making white flour, the **husk** (the seed wall) and the **germ** (the embryo plant) of the wheat are removed (see below). In wholemeal flour, the whole of the wheat grain is ground into flour.

A grain of wheat

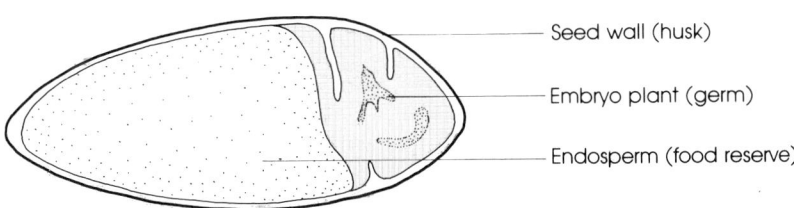

Seed wall (husk)

Embryo plant (germ)

Endosperm (food reserve)

When wheat flour is mixed with water, the proteins form a complex mass called **gluten**. Gluten provides the solid structural framework which can trap gases in the bread.

A bakery uses a large mechanical mixer.

It may hold 150 kg of flour, 100 kg of water and yeast, salt, sugar and fat. The yeast starts to act on the sugar in the dough.

The mixed dough is divided into lumps, which are put on shelves in a warm container and allowed to 'prove' or 'rise'. Then the dough passes on a conveyor belt through a hot oven.

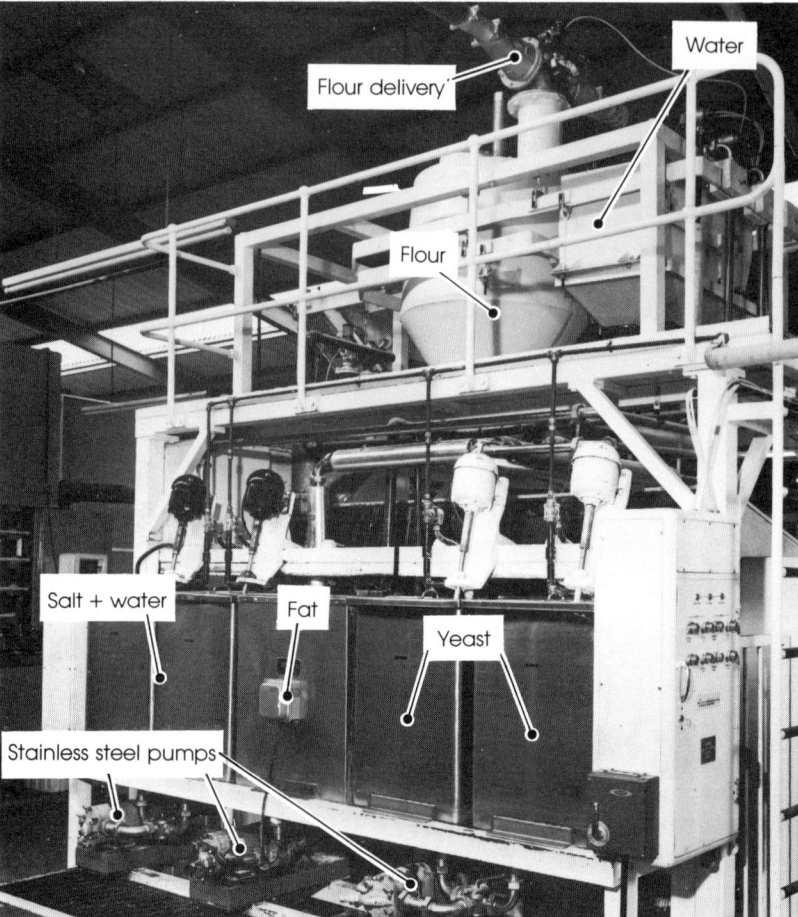

Flour delivery

Water

Flour

A mixer in the Tweedy
bakery

Salt + water

Fat

Yeast

Stainless steel pumps

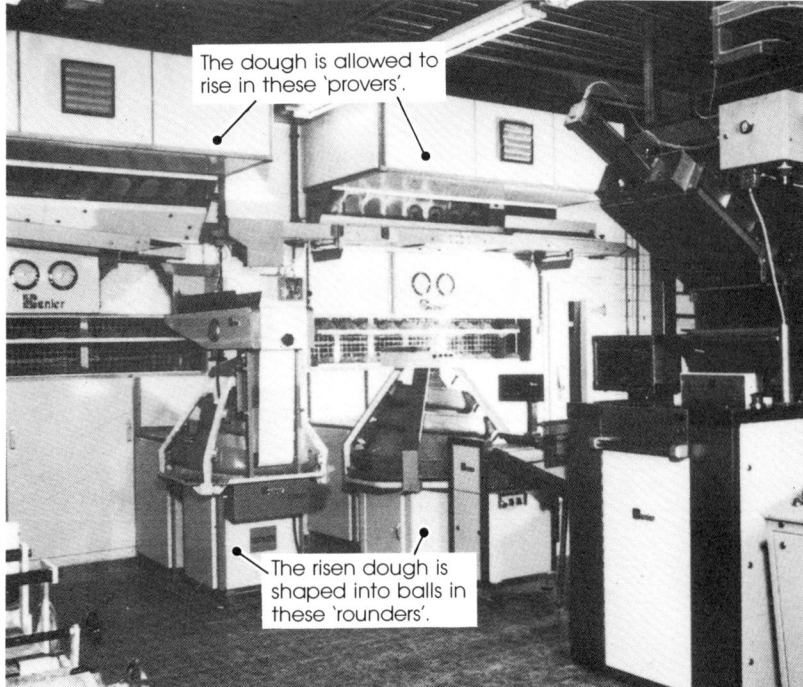

The dough is allowed to
rise in these 'provers'.

A prover in the Tweedy
bakery

The risen dough is
shaped into balls in
these 'rounders'.

The conveyor belt carries the baked loaves out of the oven. They are left to cool.

The baking properties of a flour are improved by **ageing**. During ageing, the flour becomes lighter in colour as pigments in the flour are oxidised. This bleaching, and other changes that improve the flour during ageing, can be imitated by chemical treatment. This saves money because it cuts out the expense of storing flour while it ages. Chemical ageing destroys many of the natural nutrients in flour. Vitamins B1, B2 and B3 are added to white flour to make it more nutritious. These vitamins are present in the bran (the husk) and germ which are removed when white bread is made.

**Wholemeal flour** is made by milling whole wheat grains, including the bran and the germ of the wheat. It is better for health than white flour because it contains the vitamins present in the wheatgerm. Wholemeal flour contains the cellulose present in bran. This is not digestible, but it provides valuable **roughage** (see p. 17). Wheatgerm (3% of the wheat kernel) has a high oil content. Since oil is spoiled through oxidation by air, wholemeal bread does not keep as long as white bread.

# LEAVENING

**Leavening** is the action of gases on bread dough, making the dough 'rise'. A combination of leavening agents make bread rise; they are yeast, chemical rising agents, air and steam.

## Yeast

The sugar in the dough is fermented by yeast. The carbon dioxide which is produced makes the dough rise. Some ethanol is also formed and it vaporises and assists in the leavening.

## Chemical rising agents

'Baking soda', sodium hydrogencarbonate, $NaHCO_3$, is the most important chemical rising agent. Sodium hydrogencarbonate releases carbon dioxide both on heating and on reaction with an acid. Baking powder contains sodium hydrogencarbonate and a mixture of acids.

## Air expansion

Air is trapped in the bread dough during the kneading process. As the temperature of the dough rises, the air expands and acts as a leavening agent. The volume of air increases by 27% from 20 °C to 100 °C.

### Steam production

The water which forms part of bread dough and cake batter is converted into steam. One $cm^3$ of water forms 1700 $cm^3$ of steam so the leavening effect of steam production is very great.

## BAKING

Bread is left to rise at room temperature or slightly above. Then the risen dough is put into an oven at 190–230 °C. The dough rises sharply as the carbon dioxide and the air present in the dough expand. As the temperature of the dough increases, the yeast becomes more active, and the production of carbon dioxide increases. The ethanol produced by fermentation and the water in the dough vaporise and assist the leavening. Eventually, the temperature becomes high enough to kill the yeast and fermentation stops. At the temperature of the oven, proteins and starches solidify. They form a rigid structure which traps the gases so that the bread remains leavened even when cool.

The high temperature at the surface of the bread causes browning to occur. It is due to two processes. One is sugar turning into caramel; the other is a complex reaction between protein and starch.

## CAKES

The ingredients of cakes are flour, water, fat, eggs, sugar, flavourings and baking powder. In sponge cake, little fat is used. Eggs are a major ingredient. They are beaten to make them take up a large volume of air, which makes the cake rise. A chemical rising agent is also used.

ACTIVITIES

### Making bread

Obtain a recipe from your Home Economics Department.

EXPERIMENT

### Does toasting make bread more digestible?

Starch molecules consist of long chains of sugar molecules joined together. When starches are digested, the long chains break down first into shorter chains, which are molecules of substances called **dextrins**, and then into individual sugar molecules. You can test for starches and dextrins by using a solution of iodine (1 g of iodine + 2 g of potassium iodide in 100 $cm^3$ of water).

- Starches react with iodine to give a blue-black colour.
- Dextrins react with iodine to give a brownish-red colour.
- Sugars do not give a colour with iodine.

You can use the iodine solution to compare the dextrin content of bread, thick toast and thin toast.

1) Grind up a piece of bread or toast or thin toast. Use a hand grinder (e.g. a food mincer) or an electric grinder (e.g. a coffee grinder).

2) Shake the ground bread with water.

3) Filter, using a Buchner funnel and a suction pump (see below).

**Filtering with a Buchner funnel**

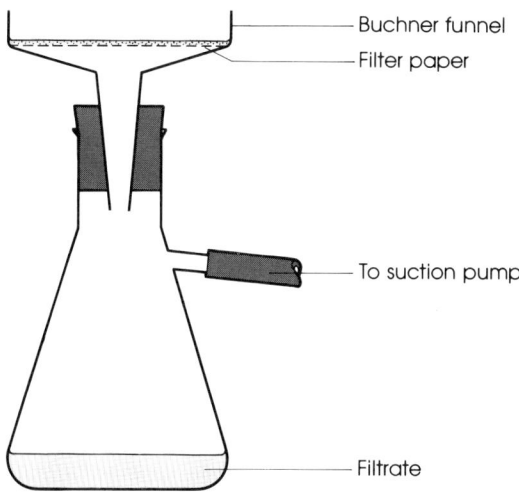

4) Test the filtrate with 1 cm³ of iodine solution. Note the colour.

5) Repeat with the other two slices of bread and toast.

6) Say which has the highest dextrin content: thick toast, thin toast or bread. Does toasting make bread more or less digestible?

## QUESTIONS ON CHAPTER 6

**1** What grain is the chief source of flour?

**2** What is (a) endosperm, (b) wheat germ, (c) gluten?

**3** What is 'leavening'? Name three common agents which are used for leavening baked goods.

**4** What are the main ingredients of baking powder? Why is it added to flour?

**5** Explain why
   (a) sugar is added to bread dough and
   (b) bread browns on the outside.

**6** Explain the difference between
   (a) wheat germ and endosperm
   (b) baking soda and baking powder
   (c) white flour and wholemeal flour
   (d) bread and cake.

## WORDPUZZLE: USE YOUR LOAF!

Trace or photocopy the loaf (see note on p. ii). Then fill in the answers to the clues.

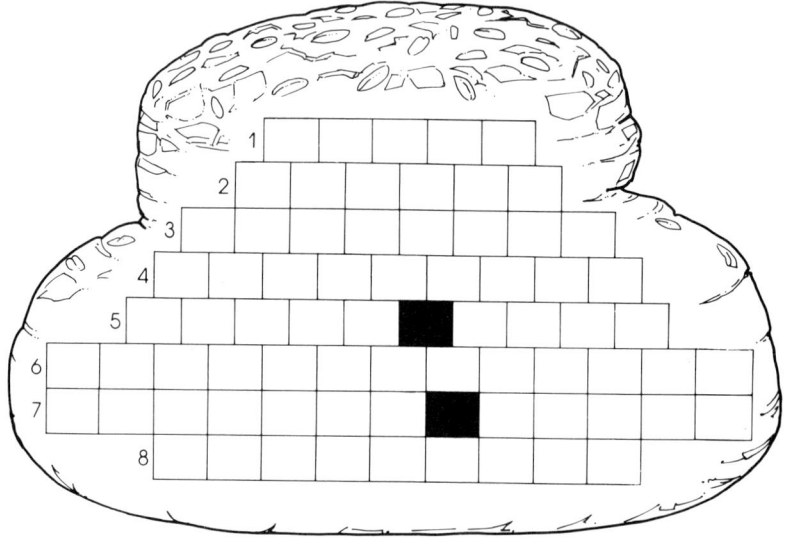

1  One of the agents that makes bread rise (5)

2  This is what makes bread stay risen (6)

3  Body-building ingredients of bread (8)

4  Needed to give dough a rise (9)

5  This is where the vitamins in bread come from (two words 5, 4)

6  Energy-giving ingredients of bread (13)

7  A part of bread which provides roughage (7, 5)

8  This is where starch is stored (9)

# MILK AND CHEESE

## MILK

The ingredients in whole cows' milk are shown in figure (a). The composition of human milk is shown in figure (b).

a)                                              b)

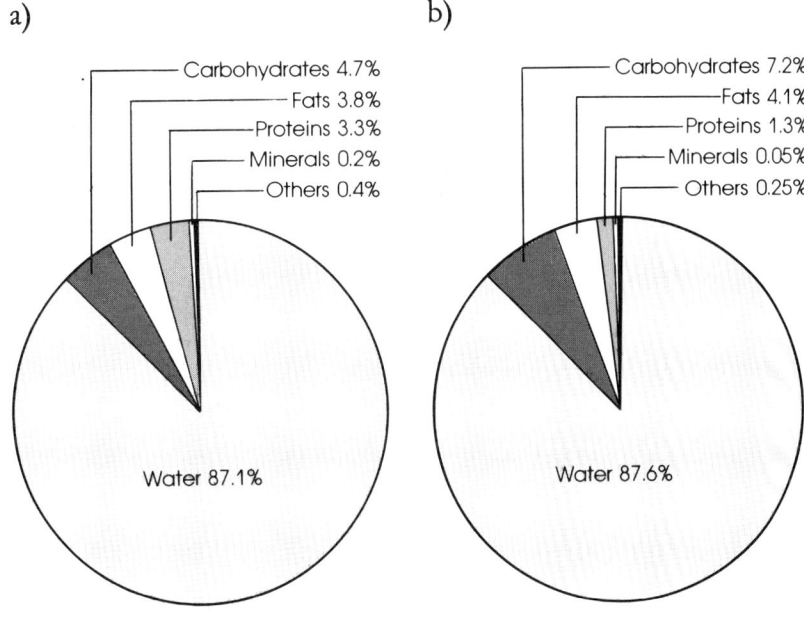

a) The composition of whole cows' milk in percentage by weight
b) The composition of human milk in percentage by weight

## Carbohydrate

The carbohydrate found in the milk of humans, cows and other mammals is **lactose**. It is a sugar which is about one-sixth as sweet as sucrose (common sugar).

## Fat

Milk is a **suspension** of tiny droplets of oil in an aqueous solution. These droplets tend to rise to the top to form a layer of **cream**. The cream can be skimmed off the milk and used as heavy whipping cream (about 35% fat) or light cream (about 18% fat) or churned to form **butter** (about 80% fat).

Skimmed milk contains 0.5% fat. **Homogenised milk** is the same all through: it does not form two layers. It is made by forcing milk through a nozzle under high pressure. This makes the droplets smaller so that they will remain suspended.

### Minerals

Many metal salts are present in small amounts. Milk is an important source of calcium compounds. Most of the calcium present is bound to protein.

### Protein

Of milk protein, 80% is **casein**. The rest is a mixture of **whey** proteins. Casein can be made to separate from solution as **curds** (see p. 64).

## PRESERVING MILK

The manufacture of powdered milk was described on p. 37. **Sterilisation** (121 °C for 3 minutes) and **pasteurisation** (72 °C for 15 seconds) were described on p. 40. **UHT milk** is made by the ultra high temperature treatment (132 °C for 2 seconds). The UHT treatment kills all bacteria. It changes the taste only slightly. **Evaporated milk** is made by removing one-third of the water before sterilising and canning the milk. **Condensed milk** is made by removing two-thirds of the water and adding sugar (45%) to preserve the milk (see p. 37). Condensed milk is unsterilised.

Pasteurised milk, sterilised milk, UHT milk, evaporated milk, condensed milk, powdered milk

## A few questions

1) Why does condensed milk keep? Why does it taste different from fresh milk? Why does it go off after the can has been open for a while? What is it used for?

2) Why does evaporated milk keep?. Why does it taste different from fresh milk? What is it used for?

3) Why does powdered milk keep well? What is it used for? How many grams of powdered milk would a manufacturer obtain from 1.0 kg of fresh whole cows' milk? (See figure on p. 61.)

4) What is the difference between pasteurisation and sterilisation? Why does a bottle of pasteurised milk go sour after a few days?
   Why does a bottle of sterilised milk keep for weeks? Why does sterilised milk go sour after the bottle is opened?

5) What are the advantages of UHT milk over sterilised milk?

6) If you wanted to ship milk to a famine area, which kind of milk would you choose? Explain your choice.

# A DIET FOR A BABY

Milk is the complete diet for a baby during the first weeks or months of life. It is an ideal food as it contains so many nutrients (see p. 61). For adults, milk is not a satisfactory diet because it contains too much water and lacks iron (see p. 61). A baby has stored iron while developing inside its mother, and this store must last until the baby begins to eat solid food.

Compare the composition of cows' milk and human milk in the figures on p. 61. Does cow's milk contain the right percentage of protein for a human baby? Does cows' milk contain the right percentage of sugar for a human baby? Is the percentage of mineral salts in cows' milk right for a human baby? Which is better for a human baby, cows' milk or breast milk?

Mothers who cannot breast-feed their babies use one of the brands of powdered milk sold especially for babies. These brands consist of dried cows' milk which has been processed to make it more suitable for human babies. Careful hygiene is needed in preparing a feed for a baby. The water added to the powdered milk must first be boiled to kill micro-organisms. The bottle and teat must be either boiled or soaked in a solution of a chemical which will sterilise them. Carelessness will allow micro-organisms to get into the feed and give the baby food-poisoning.

## POWDERED MILK FOR BABIES

Nestlé has been selling powdered milk for babies in the Third World. With a powerful advertising campaign, it has been persuading mothers to stop breast-feeding their babies and switch to bottle-feeding. The danger is that many parts of the world do not have a safe water supply. In many countries in the Third World, mothers may not have safe water for making up the feed and may have no means of sterilising their babies' bottles. The result is food-poisoning and diarrhoea. When diarrhoea goes on for a long time, the loss of water causes **dehydration** (drying out of body tissues). In severe cases, the babies fall into a coma and may die. The babies can be saved by **rehydration**. This is done by feeding the babies a solution of sugar and salt.

The World Health Organisation brought pressure on Nestlé to stop promoting bottle-feeding in Third World countries. In 1984, Nestlé agreed to restrict advertising and to stop distributing free samples of powdered milk to the mothers of newborn babies. Delegates from the Third World to the World Health Organisation are not satisfied. They point out that there is still danger from some of the convenience foods which industrialised countries export to developing countries. There is still danger that babies will be underfed on sweetened condensed milk, over-diluted powdered skimmed milk and processed cereals.

## CHEESE

'Little Miss Muffet sat on a tuffet eating her curds and whey.' What makes milk turn into curds and whey? 'The milk has curdled' used to be a common complaint in the days when few houses had refrigerators. Bacteria in the air ferment *lactose* (the sugar in milk) to lactic acid. Lactic acid (or any other acid) causes the protein *casein* to become insoluble, clot and separate from the milk as a **curd**. During the clotting, some of the lactose and most of the fat are trapped in the curd. The calcium compounds also go into the curd. The liquid that remains is called **whey**. The whey contains most of the lactose, minerals and soluble proteins.

Cheese is made from curd by bacterial action. Lactic acid formation occurs if the milk is given time to age naturally. To avoid the expense of storing milk while it curdles slowly, cheese manufacturers speed up the process. They add **rennet**, which is an extract from the digestive juices in calves' stomachs. Rennet contains an enzyme called **rennin**. Rennin helps casein to separate from solution, and clotting occurs. Cottage cheese is unripened curd from skimmed milk. Cream cheese is unripened curd from thin cream.

Curd is **ripened**, treated in various ways, to give different types of cheese. Hard cheeses, soft cheeses, sharp cheeses, Roquefort cheeses and others are all made from curd. The method of ripening decides what type of cheese is made. Ripening is brought about by a large selection of bacteria and moulds. They are spread on the surface of the curd or injected into it or added to the milk before curd formation. They bring about many chemical reactions. These changes make each cheese unique because each micro-organism provides a different set of enzymes, which catalyse a different set of reactions. Some of the fat present in the cheese is broken down with the formation of fatty acids. Many of these acids have distinctive tastes and smells, which they give to the cheese.

Cheeses

## YOGHURT

**Yoghurt** is made by the action of certain micro-organisms on milk. The milk is first boiled to kill unwanted micro-organisms and then injected with the correct micro-organisms. The micro-organisms reproduce rapidly. They feed on lactose (milk sugar), converting it into lactic acid. The increase in acidity causes some milk proteins to become insoluble, and the milk 'sets'.

### Foods to make at home

Ask your Home Economics Department for the recipes.

1) Making yoghurt

2) Making cream cheese

3) Making butter

## QUESTIONS ON CHAPTER 7

**1** If you had the job of shipping milk from the UK to a country which was suffering from famine, which method of preserving the milk would you choose? Explain your reasons.

**2** Sam, who is on a slimming diet, has decided to cut out milk and cheese completely. What advice would you give Sam?

**3** Babies live on milk for the first weeks of their lives.
  (a) Give two advantages of breast milk over powdered cows' milk for babies.
  (b) Explain why mothers who bottle-feed their babies take great care to sterilise the feeding bottles.
  (c) Explain why adults cannot live on milk alone. (Revise Chapter 2 if necessary.)

**4** What is the advantage of (a) pasteurised milk over sterilised milk and (b) sterilised milk over pasteurised milk?

**5** Make a list of all the cheeses you can see displayed in your local shops.

**6** Refer to Table 2.5, p. 25. List the nutrients which you obtain from cheese.

# CROSSWORD ON MILK AND CHEESE

Trace or photocopy the grid (see note on p. ii) and fill in the answers.

## Across

4 A favourite colour for cheese (4)

5 Add this to milk if you want cheese (6)

7 This process makes milk keep without altering the taste (14)

10 These micro-organisms are useful in cheese making (6)

11 Cheese manufacturers add an enzyme to alter the _____ of curdling (4)

14 This kind of milk has lost water (10)

15 European Economic Community (3)

17 This process will make fat separate from milk (8)

19 This process will keep the fat spread throughout the milk (14)

## Down

1 Make butter from this (5)

2 This process will enable milk to keep for a long time (13)

3 This is what the milk bottle top does to the bottle (6)

4 Same clue as 10 across (8)

6 This kind of cheese is good for slimmers (7)

8 Milk needs _____ to curdle (4)

9 There is a lot of this in milk (5)

12 The dairy farmer gets this for his milk (4)

13 An unappetising kind of milk (4)

16 Milk bottles must be this (5)

18 This kind of milk will keep for a long time (3)

# HUNGER

## STARVATION

Every two seconds, a child dies of starvation or an illness caused by undernourishment. According to the World Bank, about 600 million people (12 per cent of the world's population) are undernourished, and 15 million children die each year from starvation and disease. You have seen pictures on your television screen of children suffering from the extreme form of starvation called **marasmus**. They look like skeletons covered with skin. The children with swollen abdomens are suffering from **kwashiorkor**. They are getting some food but are starved of protein.

Why are these people starving? It is not because there is insufficient agricultural land in the world to feed all the world's population. Enough food is grown to provide each person in the world with more than they need. This chapter will try to point out a number of different reasons why people go hungry. It is in Third World countries that starvation and malnutrition are most common.

## THE THIRD WORLD

The countries in the northern continents are richer than the countries in the southern continents (except for Australasia).

The rich countries and the poor countries. The poor countries are unshaded; they are called Third World countries

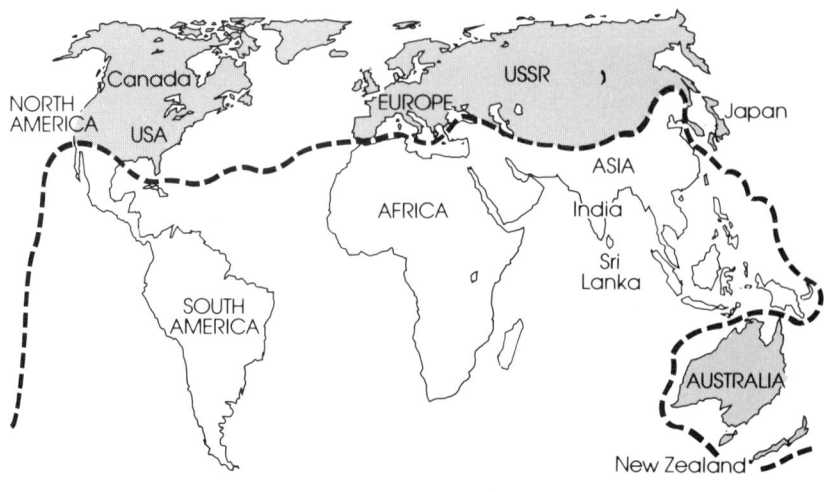

The map on p. 68 shows the dividing line between the rich countries and the poor countries. The poor southern countries are called **Third World countries**. They are also described as **developing countries** because they are only now developing modern methods of agriculture and manufacturing industries.

Most of the Third World was at one time colonised by one or other of the western European nations. In areas which were suitable for growing tropical crops, the European colonists started plantations. Sugar, tobacco, cotton and coffee were grown on the plantations, which were owned and managed by Europeans. The crops were exported to Europe. The profits from the plantations were invested in Europe, not in the colonies. The colonies developed their ability to provide raw materials for export; they did not develop manufacturing industries.

Now the colonial days are over, Third World countries have their independence. The established pattern of trade is, however, difficult to change. They still import manufactured goods and export raw materials: minerals and crops. Crops grown for export not for home consumption are called **cash crops**. Tea, sugar, coffee, cotton, cocoa, peanuts, bananas and other foods are grown as cash crops. Since 1945, the prices of raw materials have risen more slowly than the prices of manufactured goods. Third World countries have to export more to pay more for their imports. In 1984, it took ten times as much coffee to pay for a barrel of oil as it did in 1974. Many Third World countries have tried to keep up their imports of industrial equipment by borrowing from richer countries. They have run up enormous debts, on which they have to pay interest. Then they need to export more cash crops and other raw materials to pay the interest on their debts. The Sudan spends 80% of its export earnings on paying interest on its debts of $11 billion. Brazil has total debts of $107 billion.

A government needs money to spend on running the country. It has to provide schools, hospitals and other facilities. The governments of Third World countries rely on the duties on imports and exports which are paid by trading companies. Because their incomes depend on trade, these governments do not want to cut down exports of cash crops.

## EXPLOITATION

Some governments exploit their people. Many Third World countries have governments which use their income from taxes to benefit a privileged group of government employees. This kind of corruption is more common in Third World countries. In Brazil, the wealthiest 20 per cent of the population have an income 33 times that of the poorest 20 per cent; in the UK the ratio is 6; in the USA it is 11. The Ethiopian famine of 1972–4 killed 200 000 people. The government of Emperor Haile Selassie did nothing to help the starving. The BBC made a film contrasting the starving peasants with the extravagance of the Emperor's court. From the BBC film, Ethiopians in the capital city found out what was happening in the famine belt of their own country. They were so outraged that they started a revolution. The Emperor was replaced by a military government. When famine struck again, in 1984, the new government spent more on celebrations to mark the tenth anniversary of the revolution than on feeding the people.

Trading companies often exploit growers. Trading companies buy produce from farmers and ship it abroad to consumer countries. These trading companies take much of the money which the consumers pay for the food. Bananas must be eaten within three weeks of picking unless they can be kept cool. It was when refrigerated ships made it possible to ship bananas across the Atlantic that the West Indies were able to start exporting bananas to the UK and other customers. The growers cannot do business without the shipping companies which take the crop to the customers. How much of the price of a banana does the grower get? This figure will tell you.

The price of a banana (from *The Real Cost* by Richard North, Chatto and Windus, 1986)

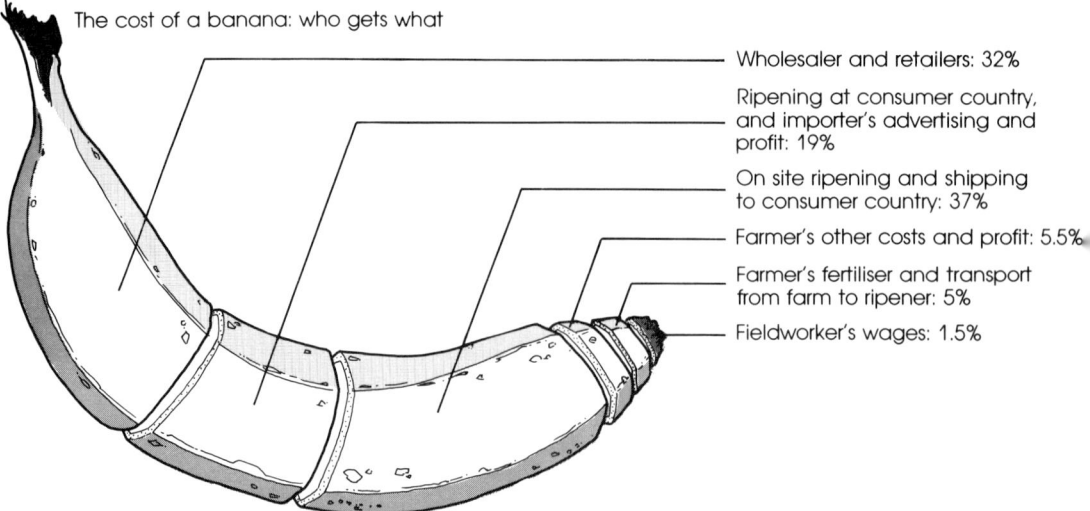

The cost of a banana: who gets what

Wholesaler and retailers: 32%

Ripening at consumer country, and importer's advertising and profit: 19%

On site ripening and shipping to consumer country: 37%

Farmer's other costs and profit: 5.5%

Farmer's fertiliser and transport from farm to ripener: 5%

Fieldworker's wages: 1.5%

Landowners often exploit tenant farmers. Scientists have bred new varieties of wheat and rice which are capable of giving very high yields. It was hoped that these new breeds would bring about a 'Green Revolution', turning deserts into farmlands. But the new varieties need plenty of fertiliser and water; otherwise the old varieties do better. Small farmers cannot afford irrigation and fertilisers; big landowners can. Poor tenant farmers go out of business, and landowners buy up their farms. They employ the farmers for a while and then buy tractors and lay off their farm workers. The unemployed have no money to buy food. The extra production is exported, and the money goes to the landowners.

Relying on one export can be dangerous. Bad weather may reduce the crop. In 1980, Jamaica's crop of bananas was only half that of the previous year because hurricanes devastated the crop. The bottom may fall out of the market. In 1975, the USA paid $1000 million to Brazil for sugar; in 1976, the USA shopped with the Philippines instead, and Brazil got nothing. In 1976, the USA bought 50% less cotton from Mexico and 90% less cotton from Pakistan than in 1975, and bought more from India. This sort of competition makes Third World countries keep their prices down. It benefits the consumer nations, but it makes it very difficult for Third World countries to plan their budgets.

## SOME CASH CROPS

### Peanuts

Mali is a country in the Sahel region of Africa (see map on p. 73). During the great drought of 1974, exports of peanuts actually increased while thousands of people starved. Peanuts are a valuable source of protein. Most of the peanut crop comes to Europe, where it is used to feed pigs and cows. European cows produce a large surplus of milk. This may be sent to Africa as dried milk for malnourished children.

### Flowers

In Colombia in South America, malnutrition is common. Fertile land is used to grow flowers for export to richer countries.

### Tea

Tea is largely a cash crop. About one million tonnes of tea are traded every year. The British drink an average of 4.5 kg of tea a year, 6 cups a day. The cost is about 1 p per cup. The tea is dried and processed in the countries where it is grown, so about half the price of the tea goes to the growers. Trading firms add 25% for blending and packaging, and 25% for transport and retailing.

The British started tea plantations in Sri Lanka (see map on p. 68) in the nineteenth century. They brought in people called *Tamils* from India to work in them. The Tamil tea-pickers live in barracks, one family to a room, which may not have even a water tap. The pay is 30 p a day for women, more for men and less for children. Many of the children are under-nourished, and many die young. A tea-picker in Bangladesh earns about 15 p a day. In Kenya, a tea-picker may earn 45 p a day.

The trading companies, such as Brooke Bond, who run tea estates have always claimed that they must make money for their shareholders. Could consumers afford to pay more than 1 p per cup? Could shareholders make do with lower profits? If the price of tea were increased or the profits to shareholders were reduced, tea-pickers could be paid the kind of rate which would allow them to live in decent conditions.

### Coffee

In Ethiopia, the best land is used to grow coffee. The plight of Ethiopia is described on p. 74. The government encourages state farms to grow cash crops, especially coffee, for export. The government spends the income on its army, which is fighting a civil war. If the income were not needed for arms, the fertile land could be used to grow food crops instead of coffee. Even during the 1984–5 famine, Ethiopia was exporting vegetables and coffee while people starved.

### Cotton, tobacco, soya beans

Zimbabwe in Africa (see map on p. 73) suffered from drought in 1984. It had to import 400 000 tonnes of maize for food. At the same time, Zimbabwe exported crops of cotton, tobacco and soya beans. Zimbabwe needs money to support its army. Would it not be wiser to become self-sufficient in food before devoting so much land to cash crops? A country which has to buy food in a hurry cannot bargain over prices. A country which grows enough food for its people can bargain over the prices of imports and exports.

### Strawberries, asparagus

Kenya (see map on p. 73) also suffered from drought in 1984. The areas with the best rainfall were in use for growing cash crops, including luxuries such as strawberries and asparagus.

### Bananas

You saw from the figure on p. 70 that the growers receive only 12% of the price of a banana. Worldwide inflation has increased the prices of manufactured goods more than the prices of raw materials. While in 1960, a Caribbean country could buy a tractor with the income from 3 tonnes of bananas, in 1970, it took 11 tonnes and in 1986 it took 22 tonnes of bananas to buy a tractor. A Third World country cannot increase the price of its bananas because the customer can buy elsewhere.

Map of Africa

THE SAHEL: THE FAMINE BELT

## IS THERE A SOLUTION?

The poor countries need more control over the price of their exports. They also need to be able to obtain higher prices for their products by processing their raw materials themselves. Sri Lanka and Kenya export tea leaves to the UK. The UK exports tea-bags and packaged tea, which fetch a higher price than loose tea. When Third World countries try to export manufactured goods, they often meet obstacles. The rich countries do not place limits on imports of raw materials. They often place quotas and tariffs on imported manufactured goods. A *quota* is a limit on the value of imported goods. A *tariff* is a tax on each imported item. The removal of such trading restrictions would help Third World countries to increase their export trade. If they are able to export more, they can also import more, and the economic health of the world improves.

## FAMINE IN ETHIOPIA

On 1 December, 1987, Bob Geldof returned to Ethiopia (see figure below). The Irish pop star was knighted for organising Band Aid, which raised £90 million in aid for Ethiopia during the 1984–5 famine which killed several hundred thousand people. Geldof wants to know why there is famine once more in 1987–8. He says that the 1987–8 famine has been caused by lack of rain and by damage to the land (through overfarming and loss of soil by wind erosion). But part of the problem, he says, is the Ethiopian government's policy for agriculture: collective farms run by the state are inefficient and unproductive. Another part of the problem is the refusal of Western governments to give Ethiopia money to spend on improving their agriculture. 'There is a ferocious famine coming', says Bob Geldof.

Bob Geldof in Ethiopia (*Times Newspapers Ltd*)

The famine is in the northern provinces of Eritrea and Tigre, as was the famine of 1984–5. In both these provinces, large bands of guerrillas are fighting the Ethiopian government. Both provinces want to become independent states, and the government will not allow them to separate. Band Aid trucks are laden and ready to go to the drought-stricken area, but fighting between the army and the rebels often closes the roads so that lorries cannot carry food supplies to the hungry.

The Ethiopian government spends £300 million a year on its

military forces. In 1977, Somalia invaded Ethiopia. After driving the Somalis out, Ethiopia now maintains a well-equipped army in case of further invasion. Russia has supplied £2 billion worth of arms to Ethiopia. The interest on this debt is £130 million a year. To pay the interest on its debts, the government needs to export. Since 1974, when the revolutionary government took over, the production of cotton, coffee and sugar has greatly increased. Food production is up only 2 per cent.

During the 1984–5 famine, the Ethiopian government continued to export fruit and vegetables to the UK and other countries. By buying these exports were we helping people in the famine areas? If we had refused to buy these exports, would the government have fed its people instead of exporting food?

## The problem

- Many people in Eritrea and Tigre face starvation.
- Their land is spoiled by overfarming and erosion.
- Large bands of guerrillas are fighting the government.
- Band Aid supplies are not reaching the hungry because of the fighting.
- The south-west of the country has good rainfall and is fertile. Very little of it is farmed at present, and there is plenty of room for more people to settle. Few people from the north want to move and settle in the south-west.
- Foreign governments will provide emergency aid but not long-term development aid.

What would you do if you were in the Ethiopian government?

What can be done to save the victims of the 1987–8 famine?

What can be done to prevent famine in the future?

This is quite a problem, and you may want to discuss it with other pupils.

## QUESTIONS ON CHAPTER 8

1 The EEC (European Economic Community) produces a food surplus. Some African countries often suffer from famine. Karen thinks that tonnes of food should be shipped from the EEC food stores to famine-stricken countries. Anna thinks this will stop African countries from working out a solution to the problems of drought and soil erosion. Who do you think is right? This is a difficult question; you may like to form a group to discuss it.

**2** During the 1987–8 famine, Ethiopian beef is being exported to the UK and other countries. Some supermarket chains are refusing to buy the meat. Why do you think the supermarket chains are doing this? What do you think should be done with the beef?

What would you do with the money from the sale of beef if you were in the Ethiopian government? What other use is the Ethiopian government likely to make of the money?

You may like to discuss these questions in a group.

**3** What is meant by (a) a *colony* and (b) a *colonist*? Why did some countries want to gain colonies?

**4** In some Third World Countries, people go hungry while their land grows exotic fruits for export. Design a poster to help people to understand how unjust this practice is.

**5** Few tea-drinkers know about the low wages of tea-pickers. What could be done to make more people aware of the exploitation of tea-pickers? What could be done to improve the lot of the tea-pickers? These are difficult questions, and you may like to form a group to discuss ideas.

**6** Herr Willy Brandt, the former Chancellor of West Germany, said 'Every minute of every day of the week, the nations of the world are spending around $2 million on armaments and military equipment. And every minute 30 children under five years of age are dying from malnutrition.' If you were in the UK government, what would you do about this?

**7** Why are many people in Third World countries poor?

Choose two statements which you agree with and two statements which you disagree with. Explain your choice.

- They are lazy.
- The climate works against them.
- They are not well educated.
- Government money is used to buy weapons instead of food.
- There are too many people.
- A few people have all the power.
- Their health is too poor to allow them to work hard.
- Most of the wealth from Third World countries has been taken by the old colonial countries.
- They expect charity from others.
- Banks and big business make too much profit out of the poor countries.

# READ THE LABEL

If you help with the family's grocery shopping, you can see the need for food labelling. With the enormous variety of foods available, you need information to help you to choose between them (see figure below). The UK has had food labelling laws for many years. In 1983, new regulations made the food industry give more information on food labels.

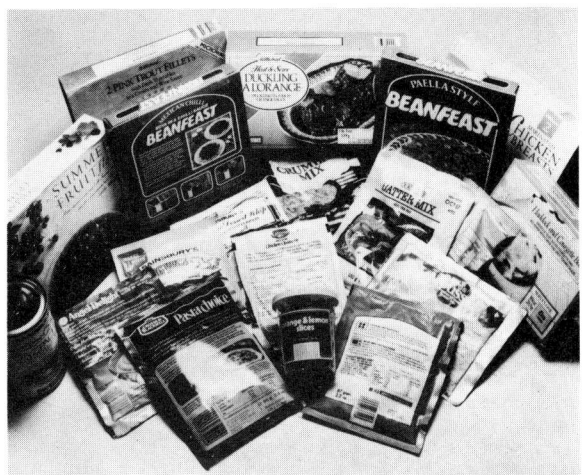

Your choice

## FOOD NAMES

All prepacked foods and almost all non-prepacked foods must show the name of the food, e.g., sugar, muesli, fish fingers. If a manufacturer gives his food product a trade name, he must add a description which tells the customer what the product is, e.g. *Nitecap* (*a malted milk drink*).

The name must not mislead the customer. If the flavour of a yoghurt comes mainly from real strawberries, that yoghurt can be called *strawberry yoghurt* or *strawberry flavoured yoghurt*. If the strawberry taste is due to an artificial flavour, the yoghurt can be called *strawberry flavour* yoghurt.

## INGREDIENTS

Labels on most prepacked foods must list all the ingredients in order of decreasing weight. Food additives are included (see p. 81). The labels on some foods (e.g. fresh fruit and vegetables, cheese, butter, yoghurt) do not have to list the ingredients.

Read the label

## NET QUANTITY

The net weight (that is, without the packet) or the net volume of food must be shown on the packet.

## DATEMARKS

Most foods must be datemarked. The datemark is based on the period of time for which the manufacturer expects the food to remain at its best. Exceptions are foods which keep for more than 18 months (e.g. frozen vegetables, spirits) and foods which are to be eaten soon after purchase (e.g. apples, potatoes).

## NAME OF MANUFACTURER

The name and address of the firm which manufactures or packs or sells the product must be given. These are the people who take responsibility for the original condition of the food.

Lyons blackcurrant fool mix

## INSTRUCTIONS FOR USE

Some foods would be difficult to use without instructions, e.g. cake mixes. In these cases, the labels carry instructions for use.

Instructions for use with the blackcurrant fool mix

**HOW TO MAKE YOUR BLACKCURRANT FOOL**

1. Pour 8fl oz (225ml) of milk into a mixing bowl and add contents of base mix sachet. Whisk with an electric mixer (high speed) for at least 3 minutes until thick and creamy (this will take longer using a hand whisk).

2. Gently fold in the contents of the fruit sachet into the base mixture.

3. Spoon the Blackcurrant Fool into serving dishes or sundae glasses.

For best results chill for one hour in a refrigerator.

within 24 hours or within 2 days if kept in a refrigerator. Equally good results using skimmed, semi skimmed or UHT
Have you tried any other
Strawberry Ch

ACTIVITIES

### Compare the goods

The two photographs above show a packet of a blackcurrant fool mix at 59 p. The following is a recipe for home-made blackcurrant fool.

**Ingredients:** blackcurrants 100 g (15 p), sugar 25 g (3 p), water 25 g (0 p), whipping cream 200 g (60 p)

**How to make:**

1) Put the blackcurrants and water into a saucepan. Cook gently for 10 minutes. Add the sugar.

2) Allow to cool. Liquidise in a food processor or with a hand whisk.

3) Whip the cream. Add the blackcurrant puree gradually, while stirring.

4) Spoon into dishes. Refrigerate before serving.

## A few questions

1) How many ingredients are there in (a) the mix and (b) the home-made fool?

2) How long would it take to make (a) the mix and (b) the home-made fool?

3) How expensive is (a) the mix and (b) the home-made fool?

4) List the nutritious ingredients in the mix.

5) Which nutrients are provided by the ingredients in the home-made fool?

6) Which of the two is the more nutritious, the mix or the home-made fool?

7) Which is the better value for money? Explain your choice.

## QUESTIONS ON CHAPTER 9

**1** Explain the difference (if any) between (a) lemon mousse, (b) lemon flavoured mousse and (c) lemon flavour mousse.

**2** 'Fado' is the name of a new food for slimmers. List all the information which the manufacturers must give.

**3** Design labels for (a) a new brand of canned dog food, (b) a new frozen pizza, (c) a new cake mix.

**4** What information is missing from the label shown below?

---

**Superfeast**

...................................................................................

**Ingredients:** Soya protein pieces, Flavourings, Dried vegetables, Modified starch, Salt, Prawns, Flavour enhancers, Colour E102, Emulsifier E322

...........        ...........        ...................
...........        ...........        ...................

**Serving instructions:** Empty the contents of the packet into a saucepan. Add 575 cm³ (1 pint) of cold water. Bring to the boil. Simmer for 10 minutes.

---

# CHAPTER 10

# FOOD ADDITIVES

'Once there was a little girl called Sarah who was pretty and blonde, and who played with her toys in the daytime. But night-time was another matter. She screamed and bellowed until dawn, flung herself against the sides of her cot and, as the months wore on, drove her mummy and daddy and a good few of the neighbours to despair.

Fortunately, Sarah was diagnosed as hyperactive before any harm was done. She was given a new diet – the essence of which was that all artificial food colourings and preservatives should be avoided at all costs.

Now Sarah's mother can keep her two-year-old daughter on the side of the angels by watching carefully what she eats. . . . A paediatrician diagnosed Sarah as hyperactive and put her on a pure food diet. . . . Any doubts as to the value of the diet were dispelled one afternoon when Sarah's father bought her a banana milk shake. "She went berserk", says Sarah's mother, "She reverted completely to her old behaviour." '

This extract from an article by Angela Wilkes in *The Sunday Times* magazine, 20 October, 1985, tells about the effect of food additives on one little girl. Fortunately, few people are as sensitive to food additives as Sarah is.

We eat some foods exactly as they are harvested, e.g. apples and lettuces. Most foods, however, go to the food industry to be **processed**, that is changed in some way to make them more attractive or different in taste and to make them keep longer. Three-quarters of the food eaten in the UK is processed. You can eat potatoes fresh from the ground at a cost of 33 p/kg, and you can eat potato crisps, which are a product of food processing, at 500 p/kg. In food processing, many substances are added. They are called **food additives**. A food additive is defined as a substance which is not normally eaten or drunk as a food either by itself or as a typical ingredient of food. Salt and sugar are added to foods but are not called additives.

No substance may be used as an additive unless the food

manufacturer can give a good reason for its use. The reasons for using additives are

- to flavour food
- to colour food
- to alter the texture of food
- to preserve food.

Additives are chemicals, but so are proteins, vitamins and all the other substances which occur naturally in foodstuffs. In 1950, 50 additives were in general use; now 3500 additives are used in our food.

The consumer magazine *Which?* reports in the May, 1986 issue on a survey of packaged foods.

'To get a general picture of the number of additives used in food, we read the labels of almost 1000 packaged foods and counted the additives in each one. Only 140 had no additives listed at all. So 85 per cent of the food we found had one or more additives. We found 28 items with 10 or more additives. The highest number of additives we found was 20 (at least) in frozen Black Forest gateau.'

Frozen Black Forest gateau – with how many additives?

## A project for you

Check the list of food items in your local supermarket. How many additives does each contain? Compare your survey with surveys done by other members of your class. You may have different figures. For example, the number of additives in pork pies can vary from 0 to 8.

List of food items:
Soft margarine, Orangeade, Vanilla ice cream, Salmon paste, Fish fingers, Sweet pickles, Irish stew, Canned garden peas, Cheese snacks, Tomato cup soup, Pork pies, Beef sausages, Strawberry jam, Black cherry yoghurt, Caramel dessert.

# TYPES OF FOOD ADDITIVE

## Additives which alter the taste of food

**Flavourings**   Flavourings are the largest group of food additives, with 3000 or so in use. The large number is not so surprising when it takes a mixture of up to 50 substances to produce a natural flavour such as apple or peach.

**Sweeteners**   The commonest sweetener is sucrose (sugar); this is a food, not an additive. Some people want to cut down on sucrose either because it causes tooth decay or because they are overweight. Diabetics cannot cope with sucrose. Substitutes are saccharin, sorbitol and mannitol.

**Flavour enhancers**   Flavour enhancers are not flavourings; they are substances which make existing flavours seem stronger. The best known is monosodium glutamate, MSG. It stimulates the taste buds.

## Additives which alter the colour of food

When food is processed, it may lose some of its colour; then the manufacturer will want to restore the original colour of the food. Forty-six colouring additives are allowed in the UK. Colourings are not added to baby foods.

## Additives which alter the texture of food

**Emulsifiers and stabilisers**   If you add oil and water, you get two layers. Some substances, called **emulsifiers**, can make oil and water mix. The mixture is called an **emulsion**. Any substance which helps to prevent the emulsion from separating out again is called a **stabiliser**. Margarine, ice cream, chocolate and salad dressings all use emulsifiers and stabilisers.

All these contain emulsifiers and stabilisers

**Thickeners**   You will see that 'modified starch' appears on many labels. It is used to **thicken** foods. It can be a main ingredient of instant soups and puddings.

**Anti-caking agents and humectants**   Anti-caking agents are substances which can absorb water without becoming wet. Many are anhydrous salts. They are added to powdery or crystalline foods, such as cake mixes and table salt, to prevent lumps from forming. **Humectants** keep products moist. They are added to products such as bread and cakes.

Which products contain an anti-caking agent? Which contain a humectant?

**Gelling agents**   To make jams, desserts etc. set, a gelling agent is added. Pectin is the commonest.

### Additives which preserve food

Food spends time in the warehouse, in the shop and in the home before it is eaten. Chemical preservatives are added to stop the growth of micro-organisms. Preservatives increase the food's **shelf-life**, the length of time the food will keep before it deteriorates. Less wastage on the shelves allows the shopkeeper to charge lower prices. Longer shelf-lives also enable shops to stock a wider range of foods so that we can enjoy a more varied diet. Some people are doubtful about whether the customer receives all the benefit of the lower prices. Some opponents of the widespread use of additives think that the savings go to the food manufacturers rather than the customers.

## CONTROLS ON ADDITIVES

It is illegal to put anything into food that will injure health. By law, all additives must be safe, that is, safe for almost everyone. Some people are made ill by some additives (see

p. 81), but then some people are made ill by some natural foods. Before an additive may be used, it must be approved by the government. The manufacturer then applies to have the additive licensed by the European Economic Community (EEC). If it is approved by the EEC, the additive is given the letter 'E' and a number. If it is approved by the UK but not yet by the EEC, it is given a number only.

## E NUMBERS

The EEC has drawn up a list of 314 safe additives. This is the numbering system:
Colourings: E number begins with 1, e.g. E150, caramel
Preservatives: E number begins with 2, e.g. E221 sodium sulphite
Anti-oxidants: E number begins with 3, e.g. E330, citric acid
Texture controllers: E number begins with 4, e.g. E461, methylcellulose.
Additives which have been passed in the UK but not yet in the EEC: number only, e.g. 107 yellow 2G; 524 sodium hydroxide; 925 chlorine

Which types of additive are present in Apricot Surprise?

Which types of additive can you see on this label?

> ### Apricot Surprise
> **Ingredients**: Sugar, Vegetable oil, Gelling agents (E331, E401, E341), Adipic acid, Lactose, Caseinate, Whey powder, Flavourings, Artificial sweetener (Saccharin), Colours (E110, E122, E102, E160a), Anti-oxidant (E320)

## ARE ADDITIVES GOOD FOR YOU?

Additives are tested for safety before they can legally be used. The tests are done on animals. They do not prove what the effects of an additive will be when it is eaten by humans in large quantities over many years. Some people believe that over a long period some additives could be a threat to health. We each eat 3–7 kg of additives a year. The general opinion among medical doctors is that additives make little, if any, contribution to serious illness.

Some foods make some people ill. When a person reacts to a food by becoming ill, the reaction is called an **intolerance reaction** or an **allergic reaction**. Allergic reactions can take the form of asthma (breathing difficulty), eczema (a skin complaint), digestive troubles, rhinitis (like hay fever), headaches, migraines, and hyperactivity (see p. 81). Many hyperactive children improve dramatically when they are put on a diet free from additives. Tartrazine (E 102), a yellow dye, is the one that is most under suspicion. It is used in sweets, fizzy drinks and packet desserts. Now that E numbers are shown on labels, if you know that you are allergic to tartrazine, you can read the labels on the foods you fancy and reject any which list E102.

Many people have become worried about the large number of additives in their food. They are looking for additive-free foods in the shops. Many of the large supermarket chains are reducing the number of additives in their products, and some firms are offering additive-free items.

## QUESTIONS ON CHAPTER 10

**1** 'I would prefer to live in a world where we harvested our foods fresh from the earth, ate them immediately and never had to give a thought to food preservatives, artificial emulsifiers and stabilisers, anti-oxidants and permitted colours. Alas, we do not live in such a world. High technology food production and elaborate chains of food distribution have created a situation in which food additives are necessary.'

This is what Leslie Kenton wrote in the foreword to Maurice Hanssen's book, *E for Additives* (Thorsons, 1984). Interest among the public in the subject of **food additives** is so great that the book is a best seller.

(a) Explain what is meant by

- a food preservative (see Chapter 4)
- an emulsifier
- a stabiliser
- an anti-oxidant (see Chapter 4)
- a 'permitted' colouring.

(b) Why does Leslie Kenton say that food additives are necessary?
(c) Why do you think there is much interest in food additives?

**2** Do you do a major weekly shopping trip in your family? Look through the week's shopping, and compile a list of additives.

| Food item | Flavour-ings | Colour-ings | Preserv-atives | Anti-oxidants | Texture-improvers | Others |
|---|---|---|---|---|---|---|
| *Example:* Yummy dessert mix | Present | E110 E122 E102 E160a | None | E320 E322 E331 E341 | E447 E401 | Saccharin |

(a) For each item on your list, say

- what it would be like without additives
- whether it would be better or worse without additives
- whether or not you would still buy it without additives.

(b) Which of the additives on your list is (a) the most useful, (b) the least useful? Explain your answer.

(c) List the foods you have bought which do not carry a list of ingredients. Why do you think these foods do not have to have a list of ingredients?

**3** Explain why many large supermarkets now have shelves of goods with a notice saying 'additive-free'.

**4** Explain what is meant by an 'intolerance reaction'. Give two examples.

**5** A ham manufacturer decides to increase the weight of the ham by injecting water into it. He needs an additive to keep the water well mixed with the other ingredients. What type of additive does he use? Who benefits from the use of this additive, the manufacturer or the consumer?

**6** How does the food processing industry help (a) housewives, (b) working mothers, (c) schoolchildren, (d) single people who cook for themselves after work?

Are any of these groups of people in danger of becoming too dependent on processed food?

# WORDPUZZLE ON ADDITIVES

Trace or photocopy the grid (see note on p. ii). Then fill in the answers to the clues. You will read a useful piece of advice in the vertical box.

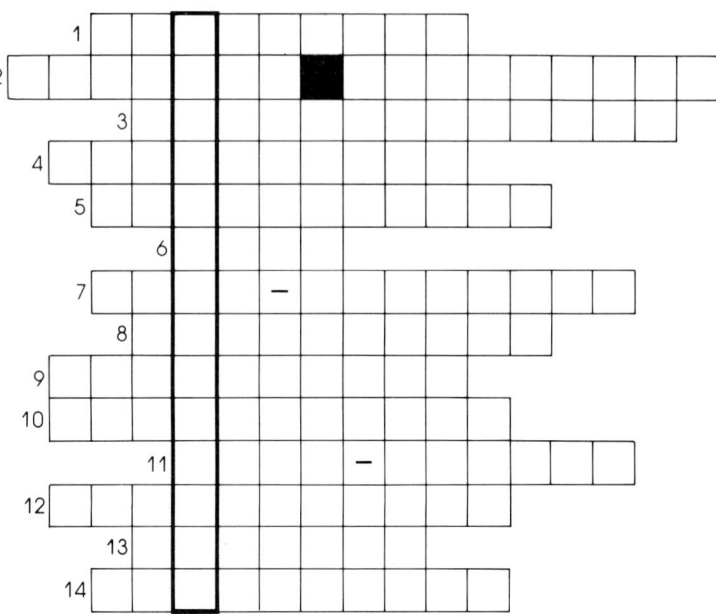

1 These do not occur naturally in foods (9)
2 These make foods taste stronger (7, 9)
3 Our food is safer thanks to these (13)
4 These are added to tart foods (10)
5 Thousands of these are added to foods (11)
6 The safety of some of these substances is in question (4)
7 These stop your salad cream from going rancid (4-8)
8 Made from starch, they are used in packet soups and desserts (10)
9 These keep bread and cakes moist (10)
10 They make oil and water mix (11)
11 These agents are added to flour and salt to stop lumps from forming (4-6)
12 They prevent your salad cream separating into oil and water (11)
13 Use this kind of agent in jam making (7)
14 All these do is to make food look nicer (10)

# ANSWERS

## Chapter 2

Questions on p. 14: 1) 105 g 2) 250 g 3) 200 g 4) 182 g
5) 140 g

Questions on pp. 23–28. 9 (a) Lost weight
because energy content of food = 4950 kJ/day, which is less
than recommended intake of 9500 kJ/day. (b) plenty of fibre
(c) No, 100 mg/day of vitamin C in the diet is greater than
the recommended 30 mg/day. (d) Short of vitamins A and
B2. (e) Eat green vegetables for vitamin B2; fat for vitamin
A. (f) No, an unbalanced diet is risky: she could easily
become short of some essential nutrients.

10   (a) and (b) energy 6350 kJ (< 9500 kJ needed),
      protein 49 g (< 53 g needed),
      fat 5.5 g,
      calcium 1300 mg (> 600 mg needed),
      iron 6.0 mg (< 12 mg needed),
      vitamin A 3.5 mg (> 0.75 mg needed),
      vitamin B1 6.5 mg (> 0.90 mg needed),
      vitamin B2 3.05 mg (> 1.7 mg needed),
      vitamin C 160 mg (> 30 mg needed).
      (c) Eat more protein, e.g., meat, fish, eggs, cheese. Eat
      foods which contain iron, e.g. liver.
      (d) Eat a balanced diet, but reduce intake of sugar and
      fat.

11   (a) Brenda 18.5 g (less); Tammy 31.0 g (more)
      (b) protein, fat, carbohydrate, minerals, vitamins.

12   *Bread and cheese*: energy 1050 kJ, protein 13.1 g, iron
      0.12 mg
      *Fish and chips*: energy 2120 kJ, protein 35.5 g, iron
      2.7 mg.

## Chapter 3,

9 (a) double (b) 1981–3

Wordsquare: toxins, enzymes, bacteria, moulds, yeasts, spore,
oxygen, colony, anaerobic, Salmonella, Clostridium, nutrients,
water, air, pH, acidic, refrigerate, thaw, ripe, hygiene.

## Chapter 5

5 (a) and (b) In 3 hours, they have drunk an average of
10 cm$^3$ of methanol – a dangerous level.

## Chapter 7

Questions on p. 63: 3 90 g

# INDEX